Pentarchy Prime Auspice Registry and Directory Libraries

The Foundation for Prime Directives and Party Declarations in Registration, Certification, Archival, and Retrieval

By

F. Dot

Completed:
December 14, 2004

authorHOUSE™

1663 LIBERTY DRIVE, SUITE 200
BLOOMINGTON, INDIANA 47403
(800) 839-8640
WWW.AUTHORHOUSE.COM

First published by AuthorHouse 02/17/05

ISBN: 1-4208-3018-X (sc)

Printed in the United States of America
Bloomington, Indiana

This book is printed on acid-free paper.

Dedication

This book is dedicated to all founders that have constructed the framework of Pentarchy Primes in preparation for all sentients to be inclusive in our transformation towards actual peace and tranquillity in the known Universe and beyond.

Table of Contents

Introduction

I am a Scribe

I am a scribe of prime importance. My journey brought me here.

One with Leprosy

I have experienced much hatred, anger, and resistance directed towards me by others due in large part to not being a believer and a faithful in the historical feudal systems. These honorable believers strongly hold onto their belief systems because they choose not to release themselves from bondage. I am treated as if I have leprosy. These honorable believers do not want to catch whatever I have. They do not want to catch higher levels of awareness and advance truths above the rampant violence that continually occur in their historical belief systems.

Time-Destiny

Some will take shots at me. Some will hit the target. I must confess. I am a big target. However, all will have to face their timed-release destiny not of their choosing.

Shared Experiences

This book is not about acknowledgment for those who came before even though I am very grateful for them. I sense that we collectively share the same experiences but in a different corporeal periods in time. Conditions have to be such for a burst of awareness to happen. Quite often, the revelation is just in front of an entity's viewing world, but is elusive for those who cannot see.

First Edition

This first edition was composed and released without delay so that the pentarchy prime founders can have a starter set in which to accelerate the premiere foundation prime construction.

This author didn't want to get in the way of sentients making initial contact with one another anxious to get started by delaying the book's release any longer than necessary. Using the instrument defined in this book will help set and quickly cure the foundation. A spectacular world awaits all of us. It is all right to be dazzled. Take care of one another and enjoy your journey.

Book Objective

The object of this book is to provide a starting point to ultimately provide a comprehensive reference instrument that completely encompasses, with minor revisions over time, the entire subject matter pertaining to the title of this book. Historical and contemporary examples and references are included to assist future auspices library duty caretakers in discovering and learning what it means to be one with others in an auspices library environment.

An Her-Storical Reference

This book in time, will be a her-storical (historical) one. It will be a snapshot as to how far we have all come from a particular point in time. For us here and now, the reference is why are we taking so long? Be patient. Changes are frightening to most inhabitants. The war they fight will be their own and not ours.

Corporeal View

To have only a corporeal view will keep one in the material realm. There is much more than meets the eye. Take a chance and see for yourself.

My Thoughts and Affirmations

The usage of the first person singular "I" in passages found in this book is of this author. "I" is also inferred in the use of "we" or "our". Readers with higher levels of awareness will easily understand the "I" to represent themselves. This author is very glad to hear this. I have someone to accompany me on my journey!

The Work that I am doing

One entity can keep the spirit flame alive and warm. So it is with the work that I am doing.

Here as a Signpost

I do not want to disturb anyone's belief system so long as it does not harm other entities self-directing well being. I am here as a signpost for any seeker who wishes information on her journey.

Strike a Chord

The reader may find repeating passages in this book. They are conveyed in different perspectives. The hope of this author is that the reader will find one that will strike a chord that will propel her into a higher awareness. This chord may cause the reader to alter her course in life so that she can encompass this higher level of awareness even more. If successful, then this author has done her part towards a sentient awareness societal domain. Has a chord been struck?

Recorded Account

This book and others by this author are provided as a recorded account describing the path towards pool consciousness.

Inner Workings

With my guidance, I can help one with the inner workings of primes.

Pentarchy Prime Background

Pentarchy Prime background is included with the discussion of auspices library. Long term, the emphasis will be primarily on auspices library caretaking.

Numerous Historical References Provided

Numerous historical references are given in this book. The are general in nature and provide starting points for anyone to research the subject matters further in order to satisfy one's yearning for complete understanding.

Similar Passages

You will identify refinements to similar passages in earlier books and editions by this author that are also found in this book.

Moderate Pace

This author functions at a moderate pace. A fast pace will just promote errors to occur in the results. Those who operate at a fast pace think that time is short for results to happen. In actuality, one has all the time in the world.

Viable Framework

I am here to pass on a viable framework whereby all can participate.

Message Heard

I am a messenger. It is up to you to hear the message. You do have a choice.

Fruitful Results

Energies for a more evolved society are ever present and will lead to fruitful results. The desire to graduate is high.

Nurturing Awareness

I am not here to evaluate the preservation of feudal states. By definition, the holdings of properties that include their subjects are inherently barbaric. The elite can choose not to be caretakers and dispose of properties at will, and often do. Allow this framework to exist no more. This break away from it will nurture sentient awareness and activities.

Written Now

This book is being written now so that when major Earth changes occur, this handbook describing non-institutional degree prime instruments will allow order to quickly be established. The instruments are non-institutional because there is no single central construct per se but are scaleable to meet each and every umbrella prime's needs.

Birth of a Framework

An initial pentarchy prime auspices library birth framework is covered in this book. Allow twenty-five continuous years with the launch of this instrument framework before making major refinements so that the framework can take hold. True, the objective is to continually develop (evolve) towards a state of a higher level of awareness. However, this will take time. Please be patient. Consider that a greatly refined framework may mean that it is not for an "Earth-based framework" but for another realm. Wouldn't that be marvelous?

Premise for this Premier Edition

Purpose

My purpose is to promote all sentients. The numbers are far greater than the members of the elite who have excluded you.

A System that Benefits No One

I do not believe in a system that condemns. This kind of system benefits no one.

As the Scribe

As the scribe, this book is being written and published so that a dawn can occur for a higher transformation to take place. In the beginning, the framework must be constructed and in place for the addition of degree prime domains in greater numbers and in rapid successions.

Set Free from Confinement

The messages are not for the non-believers who would be traumatize should these truths be made known to them. Rather, the message is for those who wish to develop in ways that can't be explained in corporeal realm. Once understood, the spirit in you will set you free from confinement. It is a wonderful feeling.

Towards Shared Pursuits

The framework described here is so that a head start can be realized for all pools to initiate their own crafting of foundations towards shared pursuits.

Choosing Proper Treatments

This book is being written now so that when major Earth changes occur, this handbook will allow order to quickly be established. Relying on arcane institutions will extend harsh pain and suffering. This is unnecessary. We have the capability to provide caring and humane treatment towards each other. Do not be fooled when others make the claim that the current belief systems are the only ones for official treatments. Dare to choose a more flexible one. With your affirmation on proper treatments, your development to the next rung towards a higher level of awareness is greater and is within your reach.

Symbiotic Relationship

The main purpose of this book is to provide insight into the establishment of an auspice library and how it is an integral part of the associated pentarchy prime's vitality. Even though it is an instrument to a particular pentarchy umbrella prime, the relationship is a symbiotic one. Neither the auspice library nor the pentarchy prime can vibrantly continue and thrive without the other.

Helping Seekers

My desire is to help seekers manage the insanity that is taking place around us.

Giving Birth

Progressing to the next level of awareness can be analogous to a mammal giving birth to a newborn. The awareness was being nurtured inside until the time of major pushes for the event of birth to happen.

Stories You will Tell

The first version of this book contains contemporary nation-state references to aid in the transformation to all-inclusive Pentarchy Prime Framework. Future book versions may omit historical references and contain post nation-state perspectives. There will be many refreshing stories to tell. Some of them will be stories that you will be telling.

Historical References on Elite Class

The Only Ones

The elite thinks that they are the only ones here. They think that we have to be quiet when we are around them so as not to disturb their dream state.

Spotting Elites

I do not know who the elites are. However, I do know their movements. Look for decisions or actions that inhibits sentient pursuits that do not interfere with others.

Right Sizing for the Few

When we embrace a historical feudal system, care for the few is the primary objective. This framework is right sized. However, the size is for the few. There is no right sizing for the masses. When we embrace a caretaker framework, then care for all is the primary objective. This defines right sizing of prime scope.

Still Kowtowing to Them

How dare we set the tone by promoting terrorism through the practice of exclusions! This is just an elitist world domination view. There are not that many promoting this view and we still kowtow to them.

In Their Best Interests

By subscribing to an elitist framework, your decisions are not being heard. In this way, the elitist will decide in their best interests. With your subscription to pentarchy prime, your leader caretakers will know what your best interests are. Why leave important decisions to surrogates (elitists)?

Derived on the Backs of the Many

The sharing of wealth does not need to be concentrated among the few. After all, the wealth was derived on the backs of the many.

Club Members Only

If you still believe in historical feudal nation-states, then ask yourself. How many members of your community are members of the elite society and how many of them will return for frequent visits to your community for advice and consultation from you? Club members only!

Support For Their Net Worth

In recent historical references, numerous business entities did not support their employee members' well being. Some supported the few within the business domains who oversaw their net worth.

Collective Ideals

The elite members want to reduce all of us to rubble by classifying us as "individuals". Dividing us into individuals enable the elite to corral us at will. As individuals, we cannot have collective ideals. Why not choose to ascend towards nexus prime?

Actions for Inactions

When executive office holders, as defined in historical terms as officials elected or appointed, claim that their hands are tied in rendering wise decision, then they may need to be replaced or placed in confinement for any harmful acts caused by their inactions.

Due to Bad Choices and Decisions

It is very disturbing to believers of unjust systems to learn that their systems do indeed exclude and hence, are unjust. These believers examine their own situations and conclude that they have privileges and freedom of pursuits. However, they cannot make the connection that they have exclusivity. These believers conclude that others who are having difficulties are due in large part to their own bad choices and decisions and that they deserve what is coming. Since the silent practice of exclusion for certain classified (labeled) members from society's good fortunes is done by the few hidden elite, the masses cannot point to these few elites for fairness. The result is that the masses fight among themselves regarding the remainder of the fortunes. Feudal systems have practiced this for centuries. We allow this practice to continue when we do not join together and create decisions and outcomes for ourselves. Your fate is in your hands. Pentarchy prime can help you.

Cold and Non-Caretaker Elitists Deficiency

A cold and non-caretaker elitist agencies and judicial systems responsible for the protection of members not developed enough to adequately take care of themselves in the societal pool and not to abuse others do prevent other members closest to them to step in and assist those members who are challenged in learning mature behavior ways. In this case, a question needs to be asked. Who are the ones who have mature behavior challenges?

It's My Party

Two extreme membership camps can be found regarding corporeal pleasures that are presently practiced. One camp finds them grand and another camp finds them offensive. Those in the offensive camp are on the offensive to pass all manners of laws making grand perspective views illegal. The larger group in the middle of these two camps is not as passionate either way on this topic. This is another example of how the few can dictate to the masses. Laws do not promote the rights of groups. It's my party!

Elite Conditioning

You will find many members of society who will claim that they are in charged of their operations. The simple truth is that they are subjects to feudal lords, which in recent historical times are the elite. If they ever were to decide on matters for themselves, they would be afraid to. This is all part of conditioning by the few. In pentarchy prime framework, leader caretakers often delegate all matters to executive duty caretakers.

F. Dot

Nothing Chic About It

There are secret societies in recent historical references containing only members of the elite monitoring the movements of the masses. They hide their existence by having the appearance and the façade that they do not exist. However, if one observes closely their movements, then one will not be mocked with their illusions. They are out in the open. Their oppression towards the vast majority is nothing chic about it.

Autonomy

The elite knows who really has autonomy. Autonomy is maintained by the vast majority in society. What the elite will do is force or shock the rest of us into thinking that the elite has autonomy.

To Serve Their Interests

Consider historical systems. The elite chooses you to serve their interests. You do not choose an elite affiliation to serve your interests. Why subscribe to this belief system? Let us choose to make our own decisions.

Elitist Stance

If a nation-state is comprised of a set of beliefs by its members who believes so strongly about its cherished freedoms and way of life, than why exclude those who wish to be admitted? Your true stated position is a terrorist one in your elitist stance. In time, your view outward will result in the view inward. This outcome can be traced back to your initial stance. The decision rests with you.

And so it is . . .

By the shaping of docile and domesticated behaviors, this is how the few keeps the masses contained and manipulated. The few want to cloud your yearning towards the notion of being a sentient. This sentient awareness jeopardizes the state of being docile and domesticated with the result of greatly diminished power for the few and the increasing power to the masses. Why allow surrogates to define your path and journey? Choose to be fee to associate in protective groups. Do not be reduced to being "separate but equal" individuals. The group is greater than the sum of its members. And so it is with All-That-Is (ATI).

Evolving Strangle hold

More and more interference with individual (entity) pursuits is the evolving strangle hold of the historical judicial systems. The premise is to shape automaton behaviors in the selection of domesticated "free" members. This behavior modification will allow them to be lead to do whatever feudal lords want them to do. All others will have their freedoms removed and be confined. The thinking is that these others cannot be domesticated and should be kept out of sight so as not to contaminate the others who are "free".

Removal is Complete

Feudal systems can no longer sustain themselves. Their premise requires the notion of property ownership to include ownership of members who are not a part of the elite. When awareness by members heightened to recognize the true mission of the elite, removal of them will accelerate. The momentum will continue towards their complete removal.

Reserved Caring

Unless there is recognition for all sentients, caring is reserved only for the few who are members of the elite pool. This exists to the disturbing naked awareness of the masses. Do not be fooled regarding the true faces of terrorists.

Foreign Sentients

Very often, the ones who will not join a foundation prime have already aligned themselves with the elite and their exclusionary societal framework. The idea of viewing all others as sentient is foreign to them. Their framework of society will crumble should any of them attempt to include others.

Scare Tactics

Historical elitist frameworks require scare tactics and methods to be deployed in keeping members confined within them. In fact, one method is to hold a large number of members in confinement for long periods of time even when no grave harmful acts have been committed. Are you one who is afraid to speak up?

Need More Persuasion

Some need more persuasion to show that the elite excludes the greater majority of members in society. You will have to ask who are the ones who are admitted to confidential and secret information? Also, who actually pay for the lion share of the elite's exclusivity? In summary, the masses are to be damned. Why do we make this so? Whose interests do the elite have as their focus?

Wears no Clothes

The royal (elite) family wears no clothes

Made Irrelevant by Choice

The historical systems of oppression on the masses by the elite will be made irrelevant. Therefore, it matters very little what artificial (man-made) constructs that do exist. You have always been free to choose your own developmental path. Choices are made for the oppression of freedom when that is your choice. How do you choose?

No Where to Hide

Laws are in place for the primary reason of keeping the elite in power and to keep the masses in check from overrunning them. To the elites, you have been advised. There is no where to hide. You will be found out.

The Wisest to the Fore

You have a choice in allowing the elite to restrict your voting to these elite few. Or you can align yourself with the active participation in the selection of leader caretakers at each degree prime. The latter promotes the participation in crafting prime directives by a greater pool of members. The wisest of leader caretakers do come to the fore and become known to everyone in this way.

Historical References on Judicial Purview

The Purview for the Few

We decorate and honor those in judicial robes for presiding over judicial review and opinion creations whether it is in the local or international arenas. This honor is done even when many years have past for the final outcomes to happen. Their false sense of their honorable legal decisions and opinions do not necessarily translate into wise ones. The championing for the "rule of law" even when great pain and suffering are present among the recipients is of no consequence when historical judicial references are made in the future. They are proud that their form of justice has been served. The true result is that justice is served for the few hard-cored believers. Wise decisions are not necessarily the outcome when the purview is for the few.

Opinions More Readily Known

Historical societies will pass laws that are difficult for non-legal members to comprehend. However, every member must comply with them and be punished when they are not in compliant. Harsh punishments are used as a deterrent for others to be aware of these laws. These legal practices are the legal profession's way of educating all members of society, which leads to legal failure over time. Revolutions occur in these situations. What ought to happen instead is the education of all members of society of impending legal status requirements. However, the profession is an exclusive closed society. Think about it. The few elite is forcing their terms on the masses. We have only ourselves to blame for permitting this to continue. Consider joining a foundation prime of your choosing. Your opinions will be more readily known.

Condemned for Life

With historical belief systems, it matters very little what life a member of society pursues after a damaging or harmful act event and resultant conviction. These historical belief systems will in high probability condemn the member for life! This happens even long after the member's release from confinement. When the "debt is paid", condemning continues by means of exclusions. Take comfort. A system that condemns will be condemned as well. You will be set free along your path towards at-one-ment.

Court Presides

This court presides over executions!

Adherence to Executions

The adherence to historical "laws" promotes the pretense for killings and executions based on them.

The Elite, of Course

Who are those in judicial and law enforcement institutions really trying to protect? Why the elite, of course!

Purview of the Few

A judicial system that condemns and terrorizes those members who have limited resources to legal (consultation) advice is not a balanced system. Where is the justice in this when it is the purview of the few?

Where is the Civility?

Regarding historical systems that can only sustain themselves through massive military personnel and weapons of mass destruction, where is the civility in them? In these frameworks, the elites choose the course pursuits for the masses to take. Normally, the course is that of perpetual wars. The masses, therefore, are properties of feudal lords that are summarily issued into service in times of war.

An Error in Judgement

A believer of the system may say that the system does not kill. An error in judgment does! However, judgments are part of the system. Therefore, the system kills.

No Qualms

The prosecution has no qualms in condemning fine citizens. This is where she fails. It leads to her demise.

The "Crime" in "Victimless"

If there are "victimless crimes" as defined in recent historical references, then why are they crimes? No victim is involved! This view is strictly a view by feudal lords on their subjects!

A Health Profession Matter

The "War on drugs" is historically viewed as a legal profession concern and not a health profession matter. The premise is to condemn and not treat members of society with the infliction. This indeed demonstrates the cruelty of the legal system. Why promote such cruelties?

Made Their Numbers

Refinements of laws, as they are historically done, will lead to more explosive entities that are not going to take it anymore. The feudal lords' solution is to incarcerate members in greater and greater numbers. Hence, these feudal lords feel that they have "made their (incarceration sales) numbers."

Built in Pricing Practices

Laws have a way of promoting and sustaining artificially set high prices.

Exclusionary Law Effect

Exclusion laws promote terror to those who are excluded.

The Law Kills

The law kills. If the law does not kill, then why do we have executions as can be found in historical references? The law kills!

One Kind of Judicial Test

The "best interest of the child" premise perpetuate imbalances in its application as observed in recent historical judicial system tests. The tests favor only the few and the masses are damned. It is strange why the masses have promoted this premise for such a long time. You can choose a new dawn and see the sunrise to a better day.

Legal Interference

Children are not properties. In recent historical time, the law interfered with the wise caretaking of children because of its need to have children be owned based on their terms. It is artificial rather than allowing natural caretakers to be involved.

Close to One Hundred Percent Success Rate

The historical referenced nation-state instrument called the Postal Service has a very high, close to one hundred percent, success rate for the delivery of all pieces of mail to the address given. The judicial system falls far shorter than one hundred percent. We are upset when mail is not delivered than when the judicial system fails to "balance the truth" with a high degree of accuracy. The law is not blind but limited by the corporeal trappings of (wo)man's biases. Know this when passing judgment.

Interim Fines

Court fines goes to whom? When there are recipients of harmful deeds, fines ought to go to them as an interim with additional costs for court services.

Compassion Up Front

The notion regarding the historical legal tool called "compensation" has built-in lengthy procedural delays. In large part, monies for legal fees must be paid first. This ensures that the legal industry will thrive and prosper. What you will find with pentarchy primes is the compassion up front in assisting those in need due to circumstances beyond their control. Those who are negligent to a high degree of certainty will have to comply with prime directives describing terms of restitution and restrictions. In this way, wise outcomes will prevail.

The Collective Known as (Wo)man

The collective known as (wo)man suits up on earth with the aim of altering the course of nature to create (wo)man-made artifacts. An example of conjoin twins is considered to be unnatural even though it is nature that created them. (Wo)man will insist that the conjoin twins be separated because (wo)man made laws require separate and distinct subjects in order to apply the laws to "individuals". This narrow view will subject conjoin twins to life threatening surgical procedures even when the vitality of both can best be maintained by remaining "joined". In mathematics when one situation demonstrates a contradiction to a postulate or theory, the entire postulate or theory is invalid. Those who believe in (wo)man-made laws cannot fathom that their laws are invalid. The truth is, they are!

Obsolete Legal Surrogates

In historical reference, there is a notion that a civilization needs a large pool of attorneys to assist in rendering decisions between members. In fact the greatest nation-state in recent historical time has a very large concentration of attorneys compare with the rest of the known world. This notion supports the premise that only the few know what is best for the masses. Why allow legal surrogates to render decisions when a large percentage of members can do a much better job? Every issue request can be right-sized.

Delays and Inhibits

Law creation and judicial decisions delay or inhibit effective caretaking activities and resolutions.

Zero Percent is Best

The laws kill, as is the current practice. It is not unreasonable to expect that this not be 100% of the time with state-sanctioned executions. Zero percent is best for any sentient society.

Innocent Spiritual Members

The historical laws allow the execution of innocent spiritual members in the societal pool.

Caretaking Omission

It is folly to believe in a framework of man-made laws when caretaker responsibilities are not defined. The belief is that laws are supreme over all. The truth is that laws cannot produce wise decision. A framework comprised of wise leader caretakers has a much greater chance in producing wise decisions. Living sentients can better handle contemporary issues. Laws produced by those who are no longer in corporeal form cannot effectively produce wise outcome in the here and now. There is only the prolonging of pain and suffering due to caretaking omission.

Boundary Laws

Law is not a caretaker construct. Justification for subservience, terror, and war is based on the set of boundary laws. Law is viewed like a machine with no sentient awareness. This is why we require caretakers be in leadership positions, which is a time honored insight.

The Essence

There are those who believe that over time, the set of historical laws will be refined sufficiently for a well tuned society. The end result is actually a society slowly going insane (mad). The society will have no sense of reality, only a sterile existence. Every member will be shaped into an automaton when artificial laws continue to inflict pain and suffering. Hence, the set of laws eventually destroys the essence of being sentient.

Harmonious Legal Bliss

There is a prevailing belief that the law is perfect or can be made perfect by passing incremental and more encompassing laws to make it so. This is folly since centuries have passed and we seemed to be in a continuous abyss in striving towards harmonious legal bliss. It hasn't happened and never will because concentration of power is reserved for the elite. Society based on the taming of the masses has made this so. Sentients with higher level of awareness will find a way out of this abyss. What is your position?

Historical References on Feudal Perimeters

Historical Outcome

"Won the fight, but lost the war." This is often the historical outcome.

Land Grabs

Nation-state constructions are part of the activities known as "land grabs". In the end, there is nothing ethical or honorable about this harmful fact.

Ancient Archeological Remains

They are truly ancient archeological remains when land is their foundation tombs and not that of a sentient foundation.

Mob Rule

In order to maintain mob rule, the edict is to incarcerate members in greater and greater numbers. A feudal system is another name for "mob rule".

Promoting Feudal Systems

The belief is that a member of a feudal system is not allowed to decide for one's self when no other member is significantly harmed based on numerous laws that are passed that pertain to this subject matter. The end result expected is that out-of-sight feudal lords have "reminded" members, who are owned by them, their relationship in society. Why are you promoting feudal systems still? Are they not in fact, feudal?

Extinction

Having the framework of nation-states forces very poor land use policies and practices. Instead of freely going anywhere on the planet and have wise land use plans that has the effect of minimal impact on Earth's resources, inhabitants have no choice than to go after land grabs and cause the savage assault on Earth. Pursuing this direction will lead to the extinction of species to include our own. The time frame is not far from the present if drastic alterations are not made. We would be wise to heed this warning.

Building a Fortress

Building a fortress for whose purposes?

Interim Fortresses

The mighty nation-state fortress is an illusion when the objective is to keep entities in or out. One need only to look at history to reveal story after story of great fortresses that were imploded and penetrated in time. They exist only as an interim.

Fortresses are built to exclude non-members. This is a classic form of terrorism. Therefore, fortresses are terrorist instruments by feudal lords.

A Shell Game

In historical references, governments are bounded by "land borders". Historical "corporations" cross all borders adhering to no single feudal government. This is accomplished by playing a shell game in transferring goods and services at will in order to dwarf the role of a single government from their share of the wealth and benefits. Adhering to land-based government elevates the stature of corporations whose officials are not elected by the members affected. Your own government will not protect you from their abuse.

Inconsequential Tale

An historical actor with the name of President Abraham Lincoln did ordered the execution of Native American Chiefs held in captivity. For him to give the order was viewed by many as inconsequential due to the designation that these chiefs are non-citizens. In truth, there is nothing glorious about this act and mindset.

Deportation

Deportation is the admission by a nation-state that it cannot exercise its responsibilities. Its role as caretaker has never been established or existed.

The "Pardon" Tool

Historical feudal lords can use the "pardon" tool on those members that have hardship convictions due to severe offenses of the past. The pardon tool is reserved for the few, mostly for the elite in society. In this way, the elite premise is preserved in this framework.

Repatriated Practices

Even in the most recent historical references, occupation armies both within and outside nation-state boundaries were forcibly "repatriated" as subjects in inhuman enclaves or forced to march towards their death. These forms of terrorism was widely "practiced" by all sides. These are indeed bleak chapters of what were perceived to be "civilized societies".

Awarded Compensation Payments

There is a notion that to heal the wrongs or grave harmful acts of the past that it is sufficient to just order the payments for compensation to the recipients of them. To those who promoted and participated in the wrongs and grave harmful acts, is this really a just outcome when they are viewed as committing no wrong doing when the payments for compensation are "awarded"? This viewed promotes the notion that the system needs only to be "fine-tuned". This is folly. It is just to hide the fact that a historical feudal system is run by feudal lords whereby members of such systems are properties of the state. Hence, the reinforcement of the system by its subjects via compensation. You can choose what you want to subscribe to. Start with your beliefs and determine what is keeping you from experiencing spiritual freedom.

Respect for a Nation

An historical reference of the late Twentieth Century is examined next. A genocide effort was taking place in Rwanda by one group of folks or faction. The world, in particular "The Greatest Civilization on Earth", could not state that a genocide was indeed taking place because that would be a legal term requiring action to be taken on a grand scale. Due to this legal quandary, the world watched as a class of citizens in a nation-state was being slaughter. The respect for a nation whose citizens are properties is more important than the respect of sentients as viewed by legal scholars. It is still being done today. The extermination of groups of citizens, this is terrorism at its zenith!

Compared to the Romans

The most recent historical supreme nation-state behaves very similar to the Romans. Its fate is no different from what they experienced. The alliance will break away one by one.

A Terrorist Rogue State

It is very ironic that the "Greatest Civilization on Earth" in recent historical time is pressuring and preventing other nation-states from having weapons of mass destruction (WMD) and at the same time, resist others in pressuring and preventing this "great" nation-state from dismantling its WMD and use. In fact, there is a notion to promote first-use of them. This "greatest civilization" was the first to use them without remorse and will do it again without remorse. How safe are you with sleeping with an elephant with a grandeur self-image? It sees no other. We can see it for what it is, a terrorist rogue state.

A Terrorist State Exposed

In recent historical reference, the "greatest and most powerful" nation-state can withdraw from treaties and state consortiums. There is nothing great or most powerful about this position. History shows that this great nation-state was not that great and powerful when it turned its back on the caretaking needs of other sentients due to these sentients being excluded because they were considered "non-citizens". The historical view turned out to be not so kind. Do not be surprised when reflections by future generations will determined that this great nation-state was in actuality a supreme terrorist state determined to have others be ruled by its feudal system ran by a few elite. It is a system that made slaves of us all. This author was present to record and expose this terrorist state. The word is now with you.

Perpetual State of Adolescence

Holding onto the framework of nation-states confines all to the perpetual state of adolescence!

Might Makes Right

The "might makes right" position or belief requires that another "might makes right" position or belief is needed to correct the wrong. This then sets into motion a perpetual bringing into the forefront another "might makes right" position or belief. Do you think that this wrong can ever be stopped? Consider removing the "might" part from the position or belief and consider reaching out instead. Consider not condemning to begin with and be caretakers for those who are having difficulties in developing as spiritual entities.

War and Terror Rights

Those feudal states that have high military machines assume that they have exclusive rights on war and terror. Time will show that their rights were in fact fleeting.

Military Adventures

There is this notion that world melding is best accomplished through military adventures. This notion is really a guise for propping up feudal systems. The true faces of terrorists are revealed.

Central Premise

The notion of feudal nation-states promotes the actions of one tribe or race to annihilate another tribe or race. This is because feudal nation-states need to have ownership of land and its resources, which translates into wealth, to sustain them and increase their holdings. The masses do not have access to these lands and are being squeezed by those few who do have access. Why is this so? It is because of our belief system to prop up feudal (land-based) nation-states. With a prime framework, land boundary construct is not the central premise, members are.

Refugee Camps

Refugee camps were illegal in the "greatest society" recounted in recent historical references. Refugees called immigrants were forced into containment centers surrounded by armed perimeters. This great society has been found to be not a caring civilization! In pentarchy prime framework, any temporary camps will have no fenced perimeters. Freedom of movement is paramount. This is defined as one of our basic tenets.

A Type of Addiction

In recent historical systems, laws are passed to shape members to do what elitists consider "proper behaviors". This promotes the domiciling of its members. The shaping promotes the notion that members are not capable or competent to do what is proper and take appropriate actions. The members then become dependent, which is similar to other types of addiction. In actuality, it is folly to think that the few know what is best for the masses. Right sizing the umbrella prime covering all parties is the best choice.

The Appeasement of Buying Power

In legal circles, to correct the sins of government for past decisions, compensation is being used to put things right instead of recognizing that the historical, distant and recent ones, form of government is to promote terrorism by the will of the elite on the masses. The premise is to buy their way out of troublesome events in order to remain in power! In other words, to appease. By placing a value on subjects by these feudal lords, you are promoting slavery. In this environment, wise decisions are not sought or welcomed. Pentarchy primes exclude no one and wise decisions are sought and welcomed.

To Qualify a Nation-State

In order to determine if a pool domain is a nation-state, one or more of the following questions must be false.

1. Is it true that the pool domain allows sentients to pass through unobstructed and stay for a time?
2. Is it true that the pool domain does not execute sentients?

3. Is it true that the pool domain gets involved with grave-harmful-acts eradication when genocidal activities are detected?
4. Is it true that the pool domain promotes the well being of all members and not just the few?
5. Is it true that the pool domain does not interfere when a member takes an action that does not interfere or impact another member?

Necessary Replacement Indicators

When great numbers of societal pool members are held in confinement or are executed, it is a clear indication that society's historical institutions are in trouble. Replacement and not the repairing of these institutions may be necessary in order for the cancer to cease its feeding on all of us. Take action when these indicators are present. Do not wait too long or the cancer grows and it then becomes a lot harder to stop.

Leaving Ruins Behind

There are those who say that a great civilization will leave behind something great. When a civilization excludes however, the things that get left behind are ruins. Those who were excluded were the ones who turned the civilization into ruins by leaving it. Is that the legacy you want to leave behind?

To Extinction

Up to and including the moment of their extinction.

Planted and Seed No More

Those who hold onto belief system relics based on feudal or land lord based framework believe that they need only plant themselves in dirt and they will last forever. What actually happens is that the dirt will cover and bury them, and they seed no more.

Property Based Contracts

There is a historical prevailing view that states that sentient interactions are property based contracts to be reviewed as such. Hence, this notion reduces sentients to property holdings by feudal lords. Sentients are not property. Promote group autonomy and allow right-sizing umbrella primes to decide.

No Need to be Stuck in Time

Subscribing to the notion that each individual is to stand on one's own is to subscribe to the notion of slavery to a feudal (land) lord. In this framework, undesirables are separated and eliminated! This includes all sentients who understand the true nature of recent historical forms of slavery. Only the wealthy land owners to include governmental nation-states have "jurisdiction" over its subjects. There is no need to be stuck in time forever. The next level of awareness can effectively be achieved in sharing and promoting pentarchy prime concerns and activities.

It is Feudal

The premise of feudal systems is just that. They are feudal systems. These systems cannot be made non-feudal. It is feudal to even try. A total replacement is needed if we are to evolve into a greater society. Won't you join me in this?

Historical References on Terrorist States

A Peaceful People Promoting Terror

If we are a peaceful people, then why are we promoting terror throughout the world with our exclusionary policies?

The War of Peace

When a member of society speaks of peace, it usually is associated with war. When a member says that another is a person of peace, it was the result of that person giving orders to the military to perform war campaigns. In time of war, no one is safe.

Root Cause

We must stop our terrorist practices if we are to have a safer world. The misplaced belief that we hold so dear to us may be the root cause for our dilemma.

Trait of a Terrorist

Condemning others is a trait of a terrorist. Why do you condemn?

Association to Terror

An historical system of laws will condemn a member of our society when she violates even one offense classified as a "felon" even when the offense involves no one else. How just is this? This type of framework promotes terror. The association to terror is not hard to make if one has a higher level of awareness.

To Give to Others

Those entities that apply their soldiers training and fighting experiences after serving the military upon returning to non-military everyday life will experience in kind that which they gave others at levels that are more severe by the judicial system. Their harmful acts are no longer sanctioned by their respective states.

An Imbalanced Time

In a historical reference, the French Revolution of the Nineteenth Century occurred when the imbalances for sentient inclusion were too great. Do we really want to wait until this event occurs again?

A Harsh Society

One will ask why I am promoting a change when I live in the most, as perceived by others, free society in the entire world? My response is that I must assist my fellow sojourners everywhere by first improving the society at large where I currently live in so that others can also be lifted. However, I tell you that a society kept afloat using the application of exclusion is a very harsh society to all.

Stopping Terrorist Activities

We need to stop propping up terrorist nation-states as the way to stopping all non nation-state terrorist activities. We need to stop terrorism in all its form.

Other Historical References for the Shift Towards a Sentient Framework

Mob Rule

In recent historical references, a system based on "for the people and by the people" is misleading when final outcomes are shaped by the elites. The election of officials in this system is based on mob rule, which is a group in chaos.

Subject to Interpretation

Beware that historical terms often are discretionary and subject to interpretation.

A Supreme System

There have been those honorable men and women who have stated that the system that they support is not infallible and still insist that all will still benefit if we continue to believe in it. In actuality, to hold on to such a system that is supreme towards "honorable men and women" will blind you and be your downfall.

A Great Nation-State That Cannot See

It appears in recent historical references that the "greatest nation-state" in the world cannot see beyond its shores. However, reception is much greater everywhere else in the world. How odd this is for a nation-state so "great" that it cannot see other nation-states that have much greater awareness of the world.

Annihilation that is Reflective

It is strange for boundary nation-states to amass great armies in their promotion of weapons of mass destruction. The purpose is the annihilation of their enemies, which is reflective.

Condemn Not

As of the writing of this book, statistics show that there are over two million members of the "greatest nation-state" in prisons at any one time. The number of law enforcement and private security personnel will show more numbers than those who are incarcerated. What a growth industry! However, are we any safer than when the numbers were of magnitudes smaller? I dare say not! The industry of condemnation breeds more violence. In order to turn this tide, condemn not!

On a Collision Course

You are on a collision course with your identified beliefs.

Behavior Modification

Behavior modification, there are numerous historical references on this topic. Pick one. Note the end result. Does it surprise you?

Trust Shattered

When my trust has been shattered, there are just too many pieces to put back together. It will never be the same.

Separated from Parents

In Egyptian history, the leaders ordered the children of the enemies to be taken so that they can be trained and shaped the Egyptian way, which caused the neglect of their parents' ways. That lesson is being carried on today.

Hollow Words

An observation can be made regarding the United States of America President Abraham Lincoln of the Nineteenth Century and a number of captured Native American Chiefs.

The executions of Native American Chiefs by the stroke of President Lincoln's quill pen set the precedence for perpetual violence in the respective nation-state framework that proclaims that all men are created equal. This proclamation contains hollow words even to recent historical times. Let us be glad that hollow words exist no more.

Super Power Model

In historical references, the American Civil War demonstrated the military's complete approach to "scorch and burn" campaigns for the rest of the world's countries to emulate. Others did follow this model. American expansion demonstrated the approach of genocide of those who were there initially for instant wealth. Others did follow this model too. In the near present/past, the approach of the "declared super power" is to eradicate belief systems that do not emulate this declared "super power" model. As is demonstrated in many references of history, the use of force by a "great society" is how victory is accomplished in the short term only to result in its own implosion in the long term. Lasting peace is made when the model described above is not followed.

Hidden Behind Compensations

With historical compensation resolutions, officials that are elected or appointed can buy their way out of bad decisions and actions. With these resolutions, the duty caretakers are kept from center stage and still allowed to continue with their poor performing duties. Hence, they are hidden behind compensation parachutes.

The Great President Revisited

How dare the "great" President Lincoln ordered the execution of Native American chiefs in captivity! How dare the United States consider Native Americans as non-citizens! How dare they view native Americans as having a value less the cattle! How dare they view Native Americans as having no claims for American soil! How dare they be allowed to continue their terrorist ways! How dare we allow all of these actions to continue!

Lead by Example

Even the "greatest military complex" must dismantle all weapons of mass destruction of any kind. A great complex must lead by example when it demands that others do so.

Hollow Government Constructs

In historical references, a perpetual belief system in hollow government constructs whereby institutions presides over society was held tightly by members of society. Under this scheme, no viable entity is held responsible for her actions and in-actions. This belief in getting "institutions" to respond to "the will of the people" is ludicrous. We require that wise caretakers be in charge.

A Historical Legend Revisited - Take Two

There is a prevailing legend regarding President Abraham Lincoln who propelled the United States to achieve unity and greatness. However, by executing Native America Chiefs who were considered "non-citizens" that can be and were executed at will without access to judicial consul or trial did leave a lasting precedence. This precedence promoted the ideal of total annihilation of any group that stands in the way of the great nation-state that President Lincoln represents. This has also been demonstrated to be true in more recent historical references prior to the implementation of universal pentarchy prime framework. This precedence is very damaging for the world at large and beyond. Are you not glad that we have gone beyond this feudal premise? There is an insight in this case. We are comforted in the knowledge that President Abraham Lincoln returned to corporeal experience as a destitute Native American. In this way, the atrocities of even a president are balanced out with a corporeal journey in a hardship-favorable environment crafted by, in this case, the president himself! One chooses the fluctuations of experiences by the crafting of her own activities.

A Small Footnote

History is full of stories of state supremacy forces that commanded obedience of all lessor state forces only to be quashed for their exclusive unilateral ways. It is no different in recent historical reference with the supremacy nation-state flexing its terrorist ways onto others in the known world. The fact is that in order to survive, elimination of its own weapons of mass destruction must be fulfilled and participation in umbrella decision-making bodies must be relentlessly pursued. Falling short of these goals will hasten implosion and its ultimate breakup. The historical referenced spotlight will be just a small footnote over time.

Sustaining a System

By believing in a system, then you sustain it. This includes even violent and dangerous ones. Why not believe in a system that bases its framework on caretaking.

How Many Incarcerations

How many incarcerations must occur before you notice that the historical system or framework is not viable for an advanced society?

Can You See the Carnage

How many executions must occur before you see the carnage? Do you think that the numbers tell the story? Would you prefer a percentage instead? Then what is the percentage of executions that must be met before you see the carnage? Can you feel their pain too?

Life Time Tags

How many incarcerated members will it take to ask if maybe we are incarcerating too many members and that our premise for incarceration is wrong? Well, how many will it take? Once incarcerated, they are condemned for life by carrying those life time tags.

All Grown Up

Historical ceremonial or symbolic events called elections are in fact mob events in the decision making process of our lives, which are limited and restricted in scope. They cannot handle dynamic and the right sizing of the needs of members. The few elites prefer it this way so that we can be contained and herded to execute their decisions and not ours. The will of the people is easily suppressed in this fashion. Are we not sentients that we permit these events to continue? Maybe we are just children. If we are not, it is good that we are all grown up now.

The Choice is Clear

Pentarchy primes have the propensity in arriving at wise decisions. Artificial court (judicial) systems have the propensity in arriving at legal decisions, which are not necessarily wise ones. Hence, the legal system is a relic of feudal systems and not designed for a sentient domain. The choice is clear.

Events that Lead Us Here

The historical reference events and related outcomes that are recorded do lead along the path towards the Pentarchy Prime Framework.

Take Comfort

Great countries fell in history because of the exclusions of others. The law of ATI prevails. A very comforting insight!

An Epiphany for a Pentarchy Prime Model

To Grasp a Greater Society

We are all made in our creator's image. While in an Earth's sphere of influence as part of our spiritually expanding experiences, we are given an environment that best meets our needs at this present time. The clues for optimum vitality are ever present. Take our body, for example. We have two hands, each having four fingers and a commanding thumb. The thumb is larger and positioned quite distinctly different from the other four fingers. The hand utilizing all fingers and the thumb can grasp extremely well many different kinds of material objects. With this observation in mind, it is being stated here without rigorous discussion or validation that an advanced quantum leap to a greater foundation society can occur by implementing the following governing framework.

Prime Degrees or Power Primes

Initiate and select on an individual entity free spirited basis an association or pool comprised of a total of five members that closely identifies with the entity based on the other members of the association or pool who share the same identification. The members agree to bind in the pursuit of achieving collective harmony and purpose. This association or pool is called the Premiere Foundation Pentarchy Prime. The more detailed mechanics for association will be described elsewhere. From the five, one representative leader will be selected to speak on behalf of the foundation pentarchy prime in matters affecting their pentarchy prime. The leader will then form an association with four other leaders at the same pentarchy prime degree to form the next ascension pentarchy prime. The members agree to bind in the pursuit of achieving collective harmony and purpose, the same premise as the foundation pentarchy prime. From the five, one representative leader will be selected to speak on behalf of the ascension pentarchy prime in matters affecting their pentarchy prime. The leader will then form an association with four other leaders at the same pentarchy prime degree to form the next ascension pentarchy prime. This process repeats until the apex pentarchy prime is achieved whereby every foundation pentarchy prime is a descendent of one of the representative leader caretakers of the apex pentarchy prime. The proper name for this prime is the Sentient Nexus Pentarchy Prime. The premise for each degree of pentarchy primes is to wisely derive decisions encompassing all members under its umbrella on matters involving two or more degree minus-one foundation primes for a particular degree pentarchy prime.

Pentarchy Prime Associations

Let's start with building blocks. They are group associations of five that are allowed to be autonomous in their affairs dealing with one another in these associations. Complete respect for a group to exist apart from other groups is a basic tenet.

Power Prime Matrices

For the foreseeable future, each pentarchy prime degrees of five member entities or groups are given in the following table.

Prime Matrix 1: 5 to the first power	= 5	
Prime Matrix 2: 5 to the second power	= 25	
Prime Matrix 3: 5 to the third power	= 125	
Prime Matrix 4: 5 to the forth power	= 625	
Prime Matrix 5: 5 to the fifth power	= 3,125	
Prime Matrix 6: 5 to the sixth power	= 15,625	
Prime Matrix 7: 5 to the seventh power	= 78,125	
Prime Matrix 8: 5 to the eighth power	= 390,625	
Prime Matrix 9: 5 to the ninth power	= 1,953,125	
Prime Matrix 10: 5 to the tenth power	= 9,765,625	
Prime Matrix 11: 5 to the eleventh power	= 48,828,125	
Prime Matrix 12: 5 to the twelfth power	= 244,140,625	
Prime Matrix 13: 5 to the thirteenth power	= 1,220,703,125	
Prime Matrix 14: 5 to the fourteenth power	= 6,103,515,625	
Prime Matrix 15: 5 to the fifteenth power	= 30,517,578,125	

Note: The primary digit always identifies a pentarchy prime with the numeral five. A Universe Prime Power Designation is used to represent each prime power degree.

Optimum Participation

It starts with an association of five to have optimum discussions and then generate decisions on matters of importance to the association. When matters deal with only the association, then that association is given the empowerment to shape the outcome of the item. All external associations will have no jurisdiction to overrule the association in question. From five associations, a higher association will be formed from the selection of one member by each of the five associations. This higher association will have jurisdiction over matters that overlap the interactions of two or more of the primary associations. When two up to five associations at the second degree have formed, then a third-degree association is formed from a member of each of the second-degree associations. Matters handled at these third-degree associations will be for items that affect two or more of the second-degree associations. This process is repeated until the greatest span association-degree umbrella can handle matters encompassing every member that is discovered. The guideline above pertains to two up to five association. It requires five associations should that number exist. In the beginning, there may only be two, three, or four associations that will formed for the next degree prime.

Prime Designation

Use "degree" prime designation to describe ascension levels of primes being considered.

From Foundation to the Nexus

The first power prime is given the term "Premiere Foundation" since all other pentarchy primes are built on this solid base. Each ascension degree association must effectively represent the number of entities given in the table above. By examining the table above, the fifteenth pentarchy prime degree represents approximately 31 billion entities! The highest degree power prime will be termed the "Sentient Nexus" because it will be closest to All-That-Is (ATI)!

Bequeathing Caretaking to the Next Ascension Pentarchy Prime

In the pentarchy primes of society, governing rules at the next ascension degree pentarchy prime involve the exchange of members in at least two of the five foundation pentarchy primes of a particular ascension prime. Another way governing rules can be defined and implemented at the next ascension degree pentarchy prime is when they are delegated by all five foundation degree pentarchy primes.

Leader Caretakers' Validation

Leader caretakers are not selected by popular vote. Validation at every pentarchy prime degree selection is required. In this way, a leader caretaker is intimately aware of concerns at every degree within her umbrella.

It is best when leader caretakers are chosen wisely.

Matters Affecting the Prime

The process of ascension (degree plus one) prime formation is repeated as long as there are still degree primes, which is to say that sufficient need to ascend even further to handle matters consisting of the nexus (greatest degree prime) for all entities comprised thereof does not present itself. Matters cannot ascend further unless a new nexus pool is discovered.

Principle of Trust

Each pentarchy prime degree association will review matters that affect its pentarchy prime because of its members' interactions pertaining to those matters. This Pentarchy Prime Principle of Trust establishes that a matter is entrusted to the pentarchy prime that is sufficient to address all parties involved. At the same time, there will be certain and severely restricted number of pentarchy prime principles or tenets that will be decreed to entrust the Sentient Nexus Pentarchy Prime because of universally recognized application.

Assignment for Greatest Growth

The assignments of duty caretakers are not taken lightly. The caretakers who take their positions in earnest will develop in ways that will not be apparent to them right away.

A Horrendous Feat

When one considers the pentarchy prime framework, one will recognize that the highest degree association of five (umbrella) domains will have been selected at each and every prime degree. This means that the sentient will have demonstrated her leadership abilities at the premiere foundation through all degrees of pentarchy primes. It is in this way that truly competent leader caretakers will be brought to the fore. This framework will ensure respect for each autonomous pentarchy prime for matters not of grave concern. More details of the process will be forthcoming as each pentarchy prime, foundation and ascension types, works them out.

Decision Appeal to Next Ascension Prime

The only time an ascension pentarchy prime will consider a matter is when one or more preceding foundation pentarchy primes issue resolutions that are considered too harsh, too extreme, or violates basic pentarchy prime tenets. Otherwise, the prime directives endure with no appeal. They are enforceable and honored everywhere. For example, debts must be repaid or in good standing before new credits are forthcoming anywhere.

To Reach the Nexus

As one is selected to the next prime degree and the next until the sentient nexus is reached, one needs only to persuade or convince just five entities, oneself included, at each degree. At the fifteenth degree, the count shows that at most 75 entities have to be convinced! This may appear to be a very small number. However, the feat is very great! The influences of nearly 31 billion entities were involved! The link to 31 billion entities is effectively communicated through 75 of them. Consider the notion that everyone who chooses or is able to participate is in fact part of the decision making process. They play a key role by selecting the best and most competent leader caretakers in their primes. These are the checks and balances that exist.

Pentarchy Prime Transfers

An advanced notification of a separation for a degree minus-one pentarchy prime from the degree pentarchy prime is permitted. Upon review of all outstanding directives and issue resolution opinions made while in the ascension pentarchy prime it is currently in, the set of terms and conditions is required for complete separation. The terms and conditions are reviewed by the degree plus-one ascension prime for fairness. Admittance to another ascension pentarchy prime with an available association slot is allowed after a transitional transfer period that is based on the particular degree prime. For example, the foundation prime will have the lowest transfer period duration than the nexus degree minus-two prime, which will have the greatest transfer period duration.

Completion of all the directives and resolutions at the moment of the transfer request must be met or is being met by the stated terms and conditions. The exception is the sentient nexus pentarchy prime since there is no other ascension prime to join!

Foundation Pentarchy Prime Resolution Submissions

When a foundation pentarchy prime submits a resolution to persuade the next ascension pentarchy prime to consider, it is up to the ascension to accept the resolution and make it effective or brief the foundation why it was not accepted for opinion inclusion. Any resolution brought to the attention of the ascension prime is considered very seriously. This information channel is the strongest link to all umbrella pentarchy primes and will ensure all are protected and viable.

Jurisdiction

Jurisdiction occurs at the greatest span degree that encompasses all of the entities involved in an issue. Bequeathing jurisdiction on a major topic item is permitted to the next ascension pentarchy prime for a period of time, for example, five years.

No Artificial "State" Framework

With primes, there is no artificial "state" framework. Our wise selection of sentients will ensure a sentient framework.

Superior Strength

The objective for a pentarchy prime framework is to simplify the decision making process in crafting wise decisions. All auspice instruments and member participation can be used in the process when deemed necessary in arriving at sound outcomes. These scaleable and simplified features demonstrate the strength of a superior framework.

Preamble to Pentarchy Prime

A Higher Awareness Charter for Pentarchy Prime

A new charter has been adopted that will aid sentients into a higher level of awareness while inhabitants in our environments. The charter for a pentarchy prime framework starts with the following preamble.

Preamble to Pentarchy Prime

It is with supreme inspiration that this sentient directing charter is drafted and accepted in order for the inhabitants of Earth and all other discovered worlds to integrate effectively, in this era of sentient awareness with one another. We understand that each sojourner is within worldly influences and at her unique level of awareness. No law is valid which states otherwise. Everyone is created equal in the realization that each one of us yearns to grow and develop in ways that will brighten the spirit-soul to the journey back from whence we came. We understand that we have lost our way and All-That-Is (ATI) has provided a way to gain back that knowledge and insight. We recognize that sentient entities have various capabilities and capacities to help and assist others in their development and that the supreme spiritual path is to be the caretakers of others. For it is by this pursuit that our journey back to ATI is assured.

Primes are for Sentients

It comes down to the basics. Primes are for sentients. The decision to partake is based on your level of awareness. You have all the time in the world. Don't wait too long. The world has an expiration date!

Prime Terminology

Sentient Characteristics

Characteristics of Sentients: The awareness that there is a collective consciousness and that self directing activities include the collaborations and associations with other sentients in excelling in quality of life pursuits and understanding.

Premier Sentient

A premier sentient is an entity with sentient characteristics who joins a premiere (initial point of entry) foundation pentarchy prime.

Sentient Zones

Different zones exist for different sentient experiences. For example, children zones are present so that they can be safe to develop into adult member designation. Another example, extreme adult zones exist where children are not allowed.

A Living Organism

A living organism is an entity that has purpose and collective awareness. For example, earth is a living organism. Earth is also comprised of other living organisms that have purpose and collective awareness.

Entity Choice for Premiere Foundation Pentarchy Prime

To select a premiere foundation pentarchy prime is a choice. Not to select a pentarchy prime is also a choice. In the latter case, a premiere foundation pentarchy prime will be chosen on an entity's behalf. Normally, it will be the final open position of five in the prime that will be chosen. Hence, their assigned premiere foundation pentarchy prime affiliation for every sentient will be known.

Devout Lifetime Partners

Devout lifetime partners are adult members who have lived and shared their lives together for more than five years.

Auspices Instruments

The construction of an auspices instrument is the result of being chartered by one or more prime directives for a particular umbrella prime. Efficiencies, economy of scale, uniformity in interpretation and fairness governance are normally the basis for the establishment of auspices instruments. They are directed and guided by one or more auspices executive duty caretakers.

Consortium Instruments

The construction of consortium instrument is the result of being chartered by one or more consortium directives for a consortium comprised of one or more umbrella prime members. Efficiencies, economy of scale, uniformity in interpretation and fairness governance are the impetuses for the establishment of consortium instruments for shared interests. They are directed and guided by one or more executive duty caretakers.

Entrance Agreement

All entities must sign and proclaim a Nexus Prime Association Agreement (NPAA) covering the essential guiding principles and tenets of pentarchy prime framework and its engaging spiritual developing and promoting environment. Ascension primes will have more specific agreement documents as primes evolve through ascension awareness.

Prime Class Time

Those entities that have expressed their intentions to join a foundation prime will be required to have an introductory class on Pentarchy Prime Foundations and then sign an agreement (NPAA) that issues are resolved through primes based on the degree-of-scope. Also, the class will cover prime directives and the importance that these crafted directives by our leader caretakers are to be complied with. Possible case scenarios regarding resolutions for non-compliance will be included.

Five Percent Trigger

Five percent of the total societal domain population that represents prime members is needed before Prime Directives can be crafted for non-prime transformation activities.

Copyright Certification

Copyright certification by a pent-n-degree umbrella prime is determined by the registration by the creator within the pent-degree tier primes. Exceptions are when clear determination can effectively be substantiated as to who the originator is or that a registry entry has been made by the originator at any auspice library of the pent-n-degree umbrella prime at least 125 days or earlier than the current originator's registry request date. A rare determination can be given to more than one due to convincing findings and fitness tests that one or more came up with the creation during approximately the same time frame.

Relative Terms:

Foundation
Ascension
Degree

Pent-Complement

A pent-complement, meaning five members or leader caretakers, is needed to form a complete pentarchy prime. Otherwise, clear prime directives cannot be forthcoming.

Degrees

Degree zero - Sentient
Degree one - Foundation Prime
Degree two - Prime Square
Degree three - Prime Cube
Degree n - Prime at Degree 'n'
Degree apex - Nexus Prime

Summit Prime

The summit prime is a prime degree view of the nexus prime.

Distinct Prime Designation

A distinct prime designation is assigned to each pentarchy prime formed based on its prime degree. The first pentarchy prime can select a particular marker name and symbol to be associated with. Others will have a suffix or prefix added to the marker name for distinction. However, a uniquely different symbol must be crafted that can be readily recognized as such. In order to be recognized with a distinct prime designation, the particular marker name must be registered and certified by the Umbrella Prime Auspice Library for the umbrella prime domain that they are to be used in. A copyright certification is generated for the marker name and symbol and recognized throughout the umbrella prime domain.

Foundation Prime Degree Zero

Foundation prime degree zero, also known as universal ground, denotes each premiere sentient.

Foundation Prime Degree One

Premiere Foundation Pentarchy Primes are identified as a prime with the designation of degree one. It is comprised of five premiere sentients.

Degrees of Foundation Primes

References in this guide refer to 'foundation primes' with respect to an 'ascension prime', which can occur at any prime degree. This refers to a reference degree for the five degree-minus-one complements of primes that form the association for the particular ascension prime.

Degrees of Separation

Prime degrees of separation towards foundation or nexus means an 'n' number of prime degrees towards the premiere foundation or the nexus.

Foundation Degree Prime

Foundation degree prime is a pentarchy prime that is a premier foundation, umbrella, or nexus being discussed as a point-of-reference.

Degree Minus-n

Degree minus-n is the number of degrees of separation from the pentarchy prime umbrella that is being referenced towards the premiere foundation prime in a pentarchy prime framework.

Degree Plus-n

Degree plus-n is the number of degrees of separation from the pentarchy prime umbrella that is being referenced towards the nexus prime in a pentarchy prime framework.

Prime Consensus

The need to reach prime consensus is every present. It means that prime directives are forthcoming and not in a state of quandary.

Pent-Degree Primes

A pent-degree prime is an umbrella prime with a prime degree designation that is a multiple of five. The primes with this designation have special charter responsibilities that are described elsewhere for pentarchy prime framework vitality.

Pent-Degree Tier Primes

Pent-degree tier primes are pentarchy primes comprised of a particular pent-degree prime and primes that are degree minus-one, degree minus-two, degree minus-three, and degree minus-four to the pent-degree prime.

Nexus Pent-Degree Primes

A Nexus Pent-degree prime is an umbrella prime with a prime degree designation that is the summit. The prime with this designation has special nexus charter responsibilities that are described elsewhere for pentarchy prime framework viability.

Nexus Pent-Degree Tier Primes

Nexus pent-degree tier primes are pentarchy primes comprised of the
Nexus Prime and primes that are degree minus-one, degree minus-two,
degree minus-three, and degree minus-four to the pent-degree prime.
If there are not sufficient degrees to form the nexus pent-degree tier
compliment of five, then degree minus-one, degree minus-two, degree
minus-three, and degree minus-four are included when needed up to the
first pentarchy prime that is not itself a pent-degree prime. This situation
can exist at any time during the continuum of the pentarchy prime
framework.

Pentarchy Prime Leader Caretakers Purview

No Single Entity Ruler

With pentarchy prime auspices and the selection process of leader caretakers, no demagogue or dictator is allowed to dominate because no single entity is permitted to rule all others.

Certification

The certification of a leader caretaker is the selection process. There is no school for this. Mentoring by present and previous leader caretakers may provide some insights for her.

Chartered with Umbrella Prime Health

Leader caretakers have supreme responsibilities for the health of the umbrella prime they are selected to.

Adept at Rendering Wise Decisions

A leader caretaker does not percolate to the nexus prime unless she is noticed at being adept at rendering wise decisions along the way and at each degree prime. This will be shown to be true.

Accountability

Our leader caretakers must account for every entity and decisions made on their behalf. They may use instruments of their own prime directive creation to assist in this.

Role of Leader Caretaker

A role of a leader caretaker is the advocacy of wise decisions on behalf of umbrella pentarchy prime members and the resolution on issues primarily brought to their attention. On rare occasions, the issues can be recognized by observations by the leader caretakers.

Leader Caretaker Supremacy

Leader caretakers are different from other classifications of caretakers. They have supremacy over all pentarchy prime domain activities performed by other classifications of caretakers. In this way, institutions can be dismantled when they no longer serve the entity pools that established their creations. Leader caretakers *do not* serve institutions. Institutions exist because of economy of scale, efficiency, and uniform quality in their results. They are mere instruments to carry out our decisions and pursuits for a better way of life.

Responsible and Accountable

The ultimate responsible and accountable caretaking is our pentarchy prime leader caretakers. They have been bequeathed access by the umbrella prime's members to any and all information and facilities under their umbrella. Leader caretakers are empowered to gain access to all sources of the truths. The auspices library is the most valuable instrument for sources of information. This is important because it aids in arriving at the best prime directives possible.

Leader Caretakers' Duties

Leader caretakers describe vision and direction, and establish policies and mission statements for the pentarchy prime, collectively, to carry out. Auspices officer duty (career) caretakers will establish the rules and guidelines, which are to be as specific as possible and allow for effective empowerment by duty caretakers. One serves at the bequest of the pentarchy prime.

Purpose of Evaluations

Leader caretakers may evaluate duty caretakers activities and the resultant outcomes. They will not make detailed decisions for them. This evaluation activity is primarily for purposes of selecting executive duty caretakers for auspices instruments. The need for them is ever present.

When Auspice Instruments are Disbanded

The pool of leader caretakers will participate in the review process of current duty caretakers when auspice instruments have been disbanded and then created anew when the need is still present.

Not Cast in Stone

Leader caretakers who create prime directives that are viewed in the future as objectionable by future leader caretakers illustrates the superior living framework pentarchy primes offers when more information is available at a later date that results in refinement of earlier prime directives. Nothing is cast in stone when a need for adjustments is present.

New Discoveries

We require leader caretakers to articulate wise prime directives when standards and guidelines are not sufficiently clear in their interpretation. New experience discoveries over a period of time will induce the revisiting and revising of existing prime directives. This is the nature of things.

Chief Prime Caretaker

One of the five leader caretakers in a particular umbrella prime can be selected to preside as a type called a chief prime caretaker when urgent matters require speedy resolutions and actions. The premise is to prevent or greatly reduce grave emergencies whenever possible.

In Time of Emergencies

There may be occasions when rapid interim crafted prime directives are needed for grave urgencies or emergencies. The umbrella leader caretakers may select one of their own to craft prime directives without the concurrence of the other leader caretakers. The duration for this empowerment is five days when three leader caretakers have made the selection, twenty-five days when four leader caretakers have made the selection, and one hundred twenty-five days when five leader caretakers have made the selection. Before the duration has ended and the urgency or emergency is still present, the continuance can be granted again using the same selection process.

Universally and Unrestricted Access

There is universally and unrestricted access by degree minus one prime leader caretakers to degree prime umbrella opinion formation sessions. The exception is when a high degree of certainty that non-protective grave harmful acts are performed by a leader caretaker. In this case, she will not be permitted to attend. Determination of grave harmful acts and resultant remedies are made by the Nexus Prime.

No Law Apron Provided

In historical view, the law can be used as an apron to shield those in positions of responsibility from performing their duties. With pentarchy prime, leader caretakers are chartered to perform these duties of responsibility. There are no aprons to hide behind.

Hardly Working

You don't have to work hard to do the right thing. Our leader caretakers will make wise prime directives when needed. They are very good at this. After all, we selected them. When we comply with prime directives, our efforts in resolving umbrella prime intersecting issues are dramatically reduced and lifted off our shoulders.

Pentarchy Prime Leader Caretakers Duration

Normal Prime Determination Leader Caretaker Removal Transition Periods

Normal degree prime caretaker transitional periods are defined for a currently serving leader caretaker when three members of a particular prime at any degree designation selects a replacement leader caretaker to take her place in serving the next ascension prime on their behalf. The currently serving leader caretaker could also be serving as a leader caretaker at a degree prime greater that the next ascension prime. The following table takes this into consideration and shows the degree prime starting with zero to be the particular prime that made the determination no matter what the actual prime degree designation in the path from premiere foundation prime to the sentient nexus pentarchy prime is. The table reflects the premise that each and every pentarchy prime can select a leader caretaker to serve on their behalf to the next ascension prime.

Selection Reference Prime Degree	Transitional Number of Earth Solar Days
0	5
1	25
2	125
3	625
4	3,125
5	3,125
Greater than 5	3,125

Urgent Prime Determination Leader Caretaker Removal Transition Periods

Urgent degree prime caretaker transitional periods are defined for a currently serving leader caretaker when at least four members of a particular prime at any degree designation selects a replacement leader caretaker to take her place in serving the next ascension prime on their behalf. The replacement is immediate with no transitional period for the currently serving leader caretaker. The currently serving leader caretaker could also be serving as a leader caretaker at a degree prime greater that the next ascension prime. The following table takes this into consideration and shows the degree prime starting with zero to be the particular prime that made the determination no matter what the actual prime degree designation in the path from premiere foundation prime to the sentient nexus pentarchy prime is. The table reflects the premise that each and every pentarchy prime can select a leader caretaker to serve on their behalf to the next ascension prime.

Selection Reference Prime Degree	Number of Earth Solar Days
0	0
1	5
2	25
3	125
4	625
5	625
Greater than 5	625

Graduated Selection Scale

From premiere foundation prime to nexus prime, leader caretakers can serve a term limit from five (Nexus) to twenty five (Foundation Degree Prime) years without the experience of a selection process event by the respective prime designation. This does not preclude a replacement selection event by members of any prime at any degree at any time. A leader caretaker whom has served a term can be selected again once a term duration limit of another leader caretaker has passed.

Term Limits

The sentient nexus pentarchy prime leaders will retain their positions for a period of five years before a new selection process occurs. Rotation of the selection process for an ascension pentarchy prime leader will occur in each of the five years, with one being selected in any given year. Re-selection is permitted. The duration for each preceding pentarchy prime degree can have a sliding scale towards premiere foundation pentarchy primes. This is to be determined by each ascension pentarchy prime.

Foundation Primes

Choice of Foundation Prime

All entities that are not confined can choose the premiere foundation prime of choice. Matters involving two or more members within an umbrella prime can defer the final opinion (decision) to a degree minus-n foundation prime that also is the umbrella prime to all parties. The view is that the opinion (decision) on a particular matter can best be handled at the more inclusive prime. An example may be due to the close proximity of the matter (issue) with the prime identified. Examples are commerce, vehicle traffic patterns, air flights, sporting events, local sanitation services, etc. A partial decision may be rendered by the greatest ascension prime with the complement portions of the final decision deferred to an umbrella degree prime closer to premiere foundation prime.

Registration Research

Entity requests for foundation prime registration can select a characteristic category type for prime selection. A list of the primes and their affinity types are compiled and provided for selection determination. Archival Auspices Libraries are entrusted with this responsibility.

Consider a Viable Selection

In considering affinity type premiere foundation prime versus geographic positional foundation prime selection, the former will demonstrate its superior viability over time.

Default Foundation Prime Selection

Foundation prime selection guidelines are imposed and enforced when an entity cannot decide her foundation prime identity. In this case, the designation prime that is determined is based on the interactions of other entities of the pent-degree prime regarding the entity in question and by the Rule of Five. Should this scenario not be easily determined, then the pent-degree prime with members in close proximity of the entity based on the Rule of Five will select on her behalf. Additional guidelines regarding more specific scenarios are described in greater details elsewhere.

Initial Prime Framework Construction Associations

Five years will be the minimum membership association declaration with their respective foundation pentarchy primes before making another selection. It is important to choose carefully because of this long-term commitment during the early years of pentarchy prime framework construction. The aim in the beginning is to learn from our experiences in the turnaround of wise decisions formed in a shorter time. After this birth and early growth period, a minimum of twenty-five days from declaration signing is given before making another selection. After this minimum period, the entity is viewed as being a permanent member.

Single Domain Association Identification

Any entity can declare and be admitted into our pentarchy prime environment from a non-pentarchy prime environment. When this happens, identification for any non-pentarchy prime association domain is not recognized. Should an entity make a request to retain her prior identification, no pentarchy prime association is allowed and restricted visitors' routes and sites are permitted only. Violations result in banishment from umbrella prime domains.

Change in Foundation Prime

Entity move requests to another premiere foundation prime are normally granted. There is a twenty-five day limitation on issues from initial notification before a different umbrella prime can review any issue regarding the entity. A twenty-five day to five year sliding scale is used as entity issue is reviewed at each step-degree umbrella prime to the nexus prime.

Prime Association Identification

A nexus universal symbol will define each pentarchy prime degree jurisdiction. A second uniquely designed symbol can be adopted by each prime of their own choosing to represent their distinctive prime identity.

Consider Rapid Turnaround Selection

One can consider proximity of prime members when joining a foundation prime. Also for prime leader caretaker, the same is true for ascension prime. This suggestion is not an absolute. However, rapid turnaround can be achieved more readily in prime review and directive crafting activities.

Prime Separation Events

When pentarchy primes are separated due to natural barriers that are beyond control of the primes, temporary inclusive domain systems are formed in order to continue caretaking responsibilities until cohesive links with the others are restored. This means the establishment of a new premiere to nexus pentarchy prime framework.

Registration of Visitors

During transformation and beyond, those who wish to visit or immigrate must register and declare their intentions. Once the immigration intent is registered and it is to immigrate, then they are given the chance to select premiere foundation pentarchy prime or are automatically assigned to one. In the latter case and once readjustment is complete, selection of a particular prime is allowed.

Ascension (Umbrella) Primes

Ascensions Pentarchy Primes

In the immediate surroundings, a premier foundation pentarchy prime comprised of five entities is formed to handle matters involving said entities. This means that if there is a dispute within the group, then it is handled by the foundation prime encompassing them. The exception will be when grave bodily or mental harm will be or has been done on any entity. All other groups will not impose their decisions on the group when matters pertain only to the group. From this foundation pentarchy prime, one entity (the thumb) will be selected from the pentarchy prime to represent them at the next ascension pentarchy prime comprised of five chosen leader caretakers who represent their respective foundation pentarchy primes. This ascension (umbrella) pentarchy prime will decide on matters involving all five foundation pentarchy primes that they represent. Areas of discussion must involve matters that overlap at least two of the five foundation pentarchy primes. This process repeats to arrive at the next ascension pentarchy prime again and again until the sentient nexus pentarchy prime encompassing every entity is formed. In the context of time, this nexus formation continually expands when more nexus primes are discovered.

Umbrella Prime Governance Reach

The umbrella prime has "jurisdiction" when the Rule of Five applies. Its rules are governed and no other prime regarding business and commerce. For all other entity issues, the umbrella prime encompassing all entities for particular issue review and resolution governance applies.

When Primes Intersect

Access routes for prime degrees affected when routes crosses, then these intersections neighboring parts of the routes are under the auspices of the greatest ascension (umbrella) prime spanning the prime degrees affected.

Direct Access to Ascension Primes

The natural progression for prime leader caretakers is the observation of the next ascension's prime leader caretakers. No restrictive rules will prevent their observations of them unless grave harmful acts have been committed or are ongoing.

Umbrella Prime Access

All leader caretakers of the degree minus-one foundation primes to a degree umbrella prime have unimpeded and unobstructed access to the first ascension prime's discussion and directive generating chambers. Access will not normally be denied to them. Exceptions are when grave harmful acts or a high degree of certainty for grave harmful acts is present.

Pent-Degree Ascension Prime

The ascension primes with degree five designation and each multiple of degree five (five times 'n' where n is any counting number) have special automatic oversight responsibilities described elsewhere. They are referred to as pent-degree ascension primes. For example, pent-degree one primes have automatic initial oversight for all pre-adult entities within their respective umbrella primes.

Completing the Pent-Complement

This rule will permit any entity to seek and find another pentarchy prime to associate with. No pentarchy prime can remain at three or fewer members for very long. Without five members, ascension cannot be made. Every effort to complete the pent-complement of five members is pursued. Temporary ascension prime association is possible due to a variety of circumstances. One such circumstance is when a member has left the pentarchy prime due to member re-selection of another prime or due to natural causes. Another circumstance is when there are no more members in the degree prime pool to pursue. Another circumstance is during times of extreme emergencies.

Foundation Primes to Ascension Prime

The immediate five foundation primes to a particular umbrella prime will have unrestricted access to the umbrella prime and its activities.

Degrees of Ascension Primes

References in this guide refer to an ascension prime with respect to other ascension primes. This refers to a referenced degree plus-one ascension prime that forms the umbrella to the five referenced degree complement of primes.

No Overlapping

With pentarchy primes, there is no overlapping or conflicting land-based feudal system set of laws. The right-sized umbrella prime has governance regarding a particular review request and resultant opinion.

False Accusations

Umbrella primes will perform discovery activities when violent accusations are made. A determination will be made. Findings of false accusations determined to a high degree will result in confinement in camps for the accusers.

Expiration for Basic Tenet Violation

For a particular umbrella prime that has been discovered to craft a prime directive for its respective umbrella that will result in grave harmful acts if fully implemented, then a greater degree prime will blocked the prime directive from being fully implemented. The greater spanned degree prime acts as an early warning or alert umbrella on prime directives basic tenet violations. A replacement prime directive stating that the original prime directive is expired and what the corrective remedies are. It will be clearly stated that all affected members are to be in compliance at the earliest and feasible moment. Those who resist will have follow-up prime directives crafted that will state degree(s) of magnitude for privilege restrictions and remedies for them. Naturally, all prime directives are archived for later retrievals and reviews.

Designation Participation Review Request

Patrons of a consortium who are in prior degree or degrees to the umbrella prime designation for the greater spanning patron domain that is sought can request designation participation review to the next prime degree or degrees. The granting will occur when the rule of five is satisfied for twenty-five days. Terms and conditions may be crafted to assist in this prime degree designation.

Promoting Sentient Well Being

An umbrella prime can heavily tax those goods and services that are viewed as relatively harmful to a sentient well being. The intent is to promote sentient well being and still permit sentient autonomy. Those same goods and services can also be withheld from pre-adult members as a way to promote sentient developmental well being.

In Time, All is in Compliance

Those historical frameworks that force servitude on other frameworks will be known throughout pentarchy prime framework as being in violation of umbrella privacy. This is to be considered a serious matter with prime directive resolution outcomes. These directives will normally describe a moratorium on reviews involving the non-compliant actors once their compliance starts. Any breach starts the clock again with severity being increased. In time, all will be in compliance.

No One is Overlooked

In Pentarchy Primes of inclusions, no one is overlooked. We all fit together in a sustainable framework. Caretaking is the key.

Every Prime Degree Step

Leader caretakers are with us every prime degree step of the way.

Measure for Measure

It will be discovered that greater degree spanning umbrella crafted prime directives are the culmination of initiatives by degree minus-n umbrella primes in their crafting of prime directives. Measure for measure, they all add up to the nexus.

Shared Prime Needs

Shared prime needs indicate the umbrella prime that is right-sized.

Incremental Participation Activities

One may view an umbrella prime with much greater degree designation spanning many umbrella primes than the less than degree designation crafting prime directives and conclude that far fewer members are crafting them. When one steps back and view things with a wider lens, wise decisions in the selection of leader caretakers were incrementally made by each member of the umbrella prime that resonated throughout. These incremental participation activities added together do create magnificent achievements and accomplishments.

Nexus Prime

Sentient Nexus Pentarchy Prime Charter

The Sentient Nexus Pentarchy Prime composed of five leader caretakers has special empowerments bequeath by all degree primes everywhere. They are chartered to ensure a safe nexus umbrella by containing all entities that have been identified as those who have in great probability caused grave harmful acts or there is high degree of certainty that eminent intent of grave harmful acts would have been done by any of them. These empowerments are of greatest importance and are universally given. The ultimate responsibility rests with them. There are and will be no other group of leader caretakers with this supreme responsibility. Naturally, a set of nexus instruments comprised of nexus auspices executive officer duty caretakers who are chartered with implementing nexus directives will be assisting in this. Checks and balances are built-in for those who abuse their caretaker positions.

Special Governance

Nexus prime has special governance pertaining to the establishment and maintenance of universal tenets and axioms. Except for early creations, new universal tenets and axioms will be shown to be rare over time.

The World's Inhabitants Agree

The Rule of Five holds with Nexus Prime as well as it pertains to business, commerce, ocean routes and use, land routes and use, sanctuaries, air, land, water quality, etc. Most of the world's inhabitants would agree.

To Fill Sentient Nexus Pentarchy Prime Positions

When less than five degree minus-one foundation pentarchy primes exist at the sentient nexus pentarchy prime degree, the remaining leader caretaker positions are selected at large by all leader caretakers associated with the existing nexus degree minus-one foundation pentarchy primes.

Propensity for Harmful Acts Doctrine

An Auspice Nexus Doctrine states that pentarchy primes are to be safe from all members with the propensity to cause harmful acts to include the extinguishing of other members. Confinement is required with no release date into the prime pool when the propensity for harmful acts still exist by these confined members.

Nexus Prime Special Handling

Grave harmful acts or issues are reviewed by the auspices of the nexus prime. The handling of all other types of cases is described elsewhere. There may be other empowerments bequeath by all primes in the future.

Reduced to Zero

The nexus rapid response teams have primary caretaker duties to rapidly reduce the extinguishing of grave harmful acts to entities to zero. Others who interfere while the nexus rapid response team is present in these situations will be viewed as participants to the extinguishing of these grave harmful acts to members. Those who are recipients of these grave harmful acts are not included in this view when their acts are to respond to protect themselves and they have suspended defensive activities.

Grave Harmful Acts Initial Investigations

Grave harmful acts can be initially investigated by degree primes in the direction of foundation primes. However, nexus prime is the umbrella prime for all-final directive resolutions and remedies. Information from the initial investigations is included in the crafting of the directives.

Nexus Pentarchy Prime Founders

The Nexus Pentarchy Prime Charter is signed by the founders encompassing the premiere pent-degree umbrella. In the beginning, there are many Nexus Pentarchy Prime founders who are unaware of the others until their interaction paths cross. We thank you for helping all of us find our way to a sentient framework void of terrorism by nation-state lords of war.

Prime Directives

Not the Exclusivity Purview

Prime directives are not the exclusivity purview of the elite. Checks and balances do not permit this in a pentarchy prime framework. You can be one of the co-creators of prime directives.

Registration and Certification

Registry of prime directives is automatically archived by auspice libraries. Research duty caretakers, whose prime directive is to investigate authenticity of registries of prime directives, which is otherwise known as certification, provide an essential viable role in the health of the umbrella prime. Certification may take additional time to complete. This is to be viewed as a good thing.

Associated Prime Registration and Certification

Automatic registrations and certifications are for those prime directives crafted at the same degree prime as the associated auspice library.

An Implementation Delay

Create prime directives when needed even when compliance will not happen in the near future. An implementation delay may be needed if it means that hardships can be dramatically reduced because of it. All will be in compliance in time. Remember, the word is eventually heard by all.

Transitional Auspice Centers

During the transitional period towards the pentarchy prime framework, record keeping of Pentarchy Prime activities will be under the Auspices of Prime Directive Libraries. During this time, viewing can only be conducted at these auspice centers.

Our Creations

Prime directives are our creations.

Creative Empowerments

Creative empowerments given to executive duty caretakers will be discovered to be effective in satisfying prime directives' requirements.

Spectacular Spread

Spectacular prime directives spread.

Spectacular Expansion

Spectacular expansion of prime directives will unfold throughout the world.

Universal Prime Rule of Five

Universal Prime Rule of Five

When more than five percent of the patrons or users of environmental resources, commerce, and business governance have association with an umbrella prime outside the particular degree pentarchy prime being considered for issue review and opinion formation, then the next ascension prime is considered. This process is repeated until less than five percent of the patrons of a business establishment or venture is not part of an umbrella prime being tested for fitness. It is a given that all patrons and users can be identified to a premier foundation prime.

An Alternate View for the Rule of Five

A different view of the Rule of Five will be given next. Both are synonymous to each other and are given to assist entities in understanding this rule using the view that can best be applied with less confusion.

Prime matters pertaining to the patrons and users of environmental resources, commerce, and business governance will be under the auspices of the nearest degree umbrella (ascension) prime closest to premiere foundation prime that encompasses greater than 95 percent of the parties (entities). Prime matters are those at the time of the issue review request. In determining the degree prime, the next degree minus-one foundation prime is considered to determine if there is not more than ninety-five percent of the parties (entities) involved at the time of the issue review request that are associated to the degree prime being considered. This process repeats until the test is satisfied. The earliest degree prime that has governance involvement when less that ninety-five percent are in the prime being considered, the immediate ascension prime is then the qualified umbrella prime for issue opinion creation.

The Rule of 95 View

A degree umbrella prime covering at least 95% of commerce or interactions among all entities will have its governance applied. Due to entity mobility pursuits, when less that five percent of entities belong to a prime domain "outside" of the particular umbrella prime satisfying this rule, no ascension interference is permitted unless an issue violates nexus tenets and universal principles.

The Rule of Five Patrons Inclusive Test

There is an exception for determining if patrons are to be included in the test for the Rule of Five. It is when patrons are guests or visitors because of the patrons' free choice. They would have given their consent to abide by prime directives while guests or visitors of a particular pentarchy prime. The definition of a guest is that the entity has been granted the privilege to stay for a longer period of time. When no guest status request has been made, then an entity is automatically given a visitor status instead and the stay is for a short period of time.

Environment and Commerce Consortiums - Governance Reach

Reach Review

Historically, businesses focus primarily on business interests. They will not normally consider macro (big picture) interests. However, prime leader caretakers do. All members affected are considered when issues are viewed.

The Rule of Five for Natural Environments

Issues regarding environments of nature will follow the Rule of Five. Otherwise, issues involving two or more entities will be reviewed and decisions made by the greatest degree prime encompassing all involved in them.

The Rule of Five for Business and Commerce

The greatest degree ascension prime identified to produce commerce and non-violent activity guidelines is the umbrella prime where the Rule of Five fitness test is satisfied for members affected by business and commerce.

Safety of Entities Supremacy

Business regulations and guidelines have no place when the safety interest of entities is present. It is the responsibility of leader caretakers to step in and diffuse any safety issue caused by nature or sentients. Also, grave harmful acts of any kind are unacceptable. In this case, rapid deployment teams will respond to this type of event.

Environment and Commerce Consortiums - Environment

The Governance Reach of Business

In regards to the reach of rules of business and commerce, it will encompass those activities where the reach is greater than ninety-five percent of the umbrella prime.

Business Patron Governance Rule

Any business that has at least ninety-five percent of its patrons (Rule of Five), including workers and employees, within a particular ascension prime umbrella will comply with the policies of said prime. This allows more degree minus-n umbrella primes, where "n" is a counting number, to have autonomy and active participation in the creation of prime directives for themselves.

Prime Governance Designation Displayed

Businesses and organizations will have prime identifiers clearly marked and displayed for prime governance. All businesses, commerce organizations, and service organizations will display and be easily accessible to all the degree prime designations whose set of business governing rules and guidelines are in effect.

Pentarchy Prime Organization Instruments

Specialized agencies charted by any designated prime will be empowered to make decisions on their own and to carry out these decisions. The designated prime has five days to decline any decision. After five days, the decision goes into affect. The prerequisite is for the agencies to forward a copy of the decision to the prime and the prime to acknowledge its receipt. Primes can not refuse receipt of the copies. Primes can choose to invalidate the decision on rare occasions.

Environment and Commerce Consortiums - Regulations and Guidelines

Continual Evolution

Viewed historically, business and commerce have gone through numerous "minute evolution moments". This will continue to be so in the future as well. However, the ebb and flow of prime directives will provide more timely responses.

Rules of Operation

Business will operate under the Rule of Five. Simply stated, the greatest degree ascension pentarchy prime that makes decisions and directives is chosen when the business or commerce issue affects at least ninety-five of its umbrella prime members. No other degree ascension pentarchy prime has oversight ownership when less that ninety-five percent are affected.

Equalizing Factor

For civil reviews and resolutions, an equalizing formula will be devised for allocation of resources between large business/commerce consortiums and prime members.

Business Rules of the Game

Business consortiums will be identified by their most ascension prime designation for the set of prime directives and companion business rules and guidelines based on the Rule of Five. All those who wish to do business in this umbrella prime must comply.

No other set applies. This premise is established for simplicity and clear identification for the rules of the game being applied.

Non-Confinement Scope

Rules and regulations pertain to non-confined members of primes not in camps or secured fortresses. Auspices executive duty caretakers are charted to formulate them.

Confinement Scope

Confined prime members have confinement governance.

Environment and Commerce Consortiums - Positions and Roles

Contact is with Executive Duty Caretakers

Unlike pre-pentarchy prime systems, institution and corporation type organizations are not the "entities" informed about prime directives in pentarchy prime framework. Executive duty caretakers are the primary entities for this information. Information includes what their roles and responsibilities are. Failure to comply can lead to their removal.

Vocation Duty Caretakers

Duty Caretakers (Pursuit View 1)

This is a general classification of caretakers that perform a set of duties promoting the safety and well being of other entities.

Duty Caretaker (Pursuit View 2)

The duty caretaker is a general classification for any role in a position whereby a skill is learned and performed in a job environment. Her duties, in whole or in part, provide a service or product for another member of a pentarchy prime umbrella domain.

Specialist Caretaker Professionals

The specialist caretaker professional is a general classification that includes specialists such as doctors, dentists, nurses, scientists, mathematicians, and a whole array of other classifications. Primarily, the distinction is the result of narrowing the pursuit of interest in an entity's sojourn.

Degree of Caretaking Duties

Minimum standards are required for caretaker duties.

Certification

Certification for non-leader caretaker positions must be met when defined by the umbrella prime.

Job Performances and Retention

Duty/executive caretakers will be measured on their performances and dynamic prime domain developmental needs. It will indicate whether or not to retain each distinction of classification for the purpose of certification or be de-classified.

F. Dot

Vocation Duty Caretaker Removals in General

Leader caretakers will make decisions in matters of removals due to serious violations by a vocation duty caretaker in any category. They will make the suggestion for the vocation duty caretaker to resign before a more drastic opinion is issued to remove the caretaker from her position with serious consequences. Serious consequences can include the added provision that no holding of the same or similar caretaker positions from five up to twenty-five years depending on severity of the offense or refusal to step down.

The objective is to get the duty caretaker to leave her position in the most expeditious manner when the duty caretakers in charge failed to follow prime directives.

Non-Compliant Caretaker

The objective regarding the general classification of caretakers who violate prime directives is to remove them from positions and related privileges. Fines can be fixed amounts or be a percentage of an assessment. Usage of a fixed percentage will be found to be more equitable for all those who are in serious violations. Usage of fixed amounts is best for minor offenses.

Sabbatical Decree

The sabbatical decree duration from holding a position once a decision is made for an entity's removal will commence five days after stepping down. This decree is specified in a prime directive or an auspices executive duty caretaker's directive.

Natural Environment-Based Caretakers

Natural environment-based caretakers will be registered with the umbrella prime based on the Rule of Five. Support packages are provided when their missions are for the greater good of the umbrella prime. It may be necessary to rotate all whom desire to participate when resources are fixed in amount. Natural environment-based executive caretakers will be identified to hold these long-term positions. They will be selected based on their skills and abilities matching the positions' qualifications.

Peace Duty Caretaker - A Bold Challenge

While in service to nexus prime, peace duty caretakers of the Nexus Rapid Response Teams will discover divine inspiration when rules and guidelines of conduct are followed to its supreme intent. In short, your graduation to a higher level of awareness is assured. This is not an easy vocation but one that will provide deep insights into ATI. Do you have resolve in accepting this challenge?

Officer Duty Caretakers Responsibilities

Leader caretakers selected by particular pentarchy primes do not normally establish the detail rules or the monitoring of daily activities. They appoint executive officer duty caretakers to carry out responsibilities for the care of the general public. Removal of an executive officer duty caretaker is done with four out of five leader caretaker opinions of the pentarchy prime umbrella. Otherwise, the same rules set forth by executive officer duty caretakers are to be followed by everyone under the umbrella. For demonstration of support, umbrella prime leader caretakers are included with the rule set compliance.

Access to Information

Duty caretakers will keep no information secret when the information serves a vital prime domain interest or the well being of all. All information will be available to leader caretakers without restrictions. Failure by knowingly withholding essential information by duty caretakers is a serious offense that will normally lead to immediate removal of caretaker duties and restrictions on similar positions in the future.

Review and Remedy Duty Caretakers

This is a classification of caretakers, historically known as court judges, that presides in matters that require review and resolution activities for disputed issues brought to the Auspices Review and Remedy Instruments by members of the community. These issues are not to be of the most serious kind, which are specifically the responsibilities of the sentient nexus pentarchy prime and auspices instruments.

Advisory Duty Caretakers

Advisory duty caretaker is a classification of caretakers that work in an advisory capacity in promoting the implementation of prime directives.

Scribe Caretakers Needed

Throughout history, scribes recorded the events and decisions of their time. This made it possible to form the basis regarding later decisions when their writings were consulted. However in historical times, the premise was to maintain terrorist nation-states.

Today, scribe caretakers are needed in a pentarchy prime framework because wise leader caretakers will wisely consult and review archival prime directives to more effectively craft the best prime directives of the present day.

Confinement Duty Caretakers Needed

Confinement duty caretakers are needed for those in confinement. Locking up members and "throwing away the key" is not a premise in a sentient society. An urgent errand on behalf of the confined member is a responsibility of this duty caretaker.

Interested Developmental Caretaker

When there is no foul play by an interested child developmental caretaker in the caretaking of a child for a significant period of time, she may request and normally is permitted to be one of the five designated core developmental caretakers. More than one is better.

Not a Given

Pre-adult duty caretaker status is not a given but is evaluated by pent-degree umbrella primes. The highest level of interest on behalf of pre-adult members is the central theme for arriving at wise opinions.

Loosing Sight

When we as a society condemn, we loose sight of being caretakers. This will cloud our view and our actions. Without putting caretaking activities primary, how can society survive and be vibrant?

Taking Up the Calling

Allow your caretakers the support they need to effectively help you. If you object to their crafted directives, rules, and guidelines, then consider taking up the calling yourself. You will discover that wise decisions will promote wise agendas and pursuits.

Duty Caretakers Respected

Duty caretakers are to be respected provided sincere efforts by them are made. Consider being their mentor.

Executive Duty Caretakers

Executive Duty Caretakers

This is a duty caretaker classification of caretakers that effectively oversee the vision and operation of an organization or association instrument.

Term Limits for Executive Duty Caretakers

There are no term limits for non-auspices executive duty caretakers. Removal is possible when there exists a pattern of failing to comply with one or more prime directives.

Of Essence and Spirit

Leader caretakers will direct executive duty caretakers to carry out the essence and spirit of Prime Directives.

In Check

Prime directives will keep all in check. The directives are given to executive duty caretakers and not artificial constructs such as institutions or agencies. In this way, roles and responsibilities are assigned to duty caretakers to carry out the directives. Failure to comply will lead to removal of executive duty caretakers and the selection of their replacements.

Executive Duty Caretaker Accountability

Executive duty caretakers will be given the accountability to execute and oversee day-to-day matters regarding an auspice instrument. At times when matters are not wisely crafted and delivered by duty caretakers, these executive duty caretakers have the responsibility in making them so. There may be situations when requests for opinion by umbrella pentarchy prime are wisely pursued for clarity and direction.

Reduced Impact Time to Implement

Executive duty caretakers will inform leader caretakers if more time to implement a prime directive is advantageous in the long term with revised projected reduced impact conclusion is great.

Prime Auspices Executive Duty Caretaker

Auspices Executive Duty Caretakers

This is a duty caretaker classification of caretakers that effectively oversee the auspices of an ascension pentarchy prime instrument. She serves at the pleasure of the ascension pentarchy prime and her skills and abilities are key factors in the prime's selection.

Auspices Executive Duty Caretakers Charter

The auspices executive duty caretakers are empowered to implement prime directives assigned to them. The prime directives may be general or quite specific. When general, they are chartered with the responsibility for producing the detailed specifications and then implementing them. The umbrella prime that these caretakers serve will be provided with adequate resources to accomplish their directives.

Auspices Prime Secretary

An auspices prime secretary -- a unique classification distinction among auspices executive duty caretakers -- has the honor and duty of recording prime directives. Her duties include the safekeeping of the prime directives for posterity and the submission of copies of them to pent-degree archival recording centers.

Term Limits for Auspices Executive Duty Caretakers

There is no pre-set term limits for auspices executive duty caretakers. To be removed from this position on the opinion of the respective pentarchy prime is not to be considered an offense. To violate one's own body of rules set forth for all in the domain under her care is considered to be a serious offense. In this case, the highest penalties and/or exclusions will be imposed for such offenses. After all, an executive duty caretaker knows what is or is not an offense and will be held to the highest standards.

Removal of Auspices Executive Duty Caretakers

Removal of an auspices executive duty caretaker holding a particular position requires three leader caretaker opinions for normal ending duration. This duration allows for a transitional period before another selected auspices executive duty caretaker to assume this position. For immediate removal requires four or more leader caretaker opinions. The latter action would normally occur for serious duty violations or the failure to comply with prime directives. The umbrella prime that these caretakers serve will be provided with adequate resources to accomplish their directives.

Executive Duty Caretakers Duration

Prime directives can empower auspices executive duty caretakers that are selected to define guidelines and penalties pertaining to the set of declarations defined in prime directives. Their duty duration can have expiration dates or they can be replaced when they have abused or significantly deviated from the defined set of declarations.

Nexus Rapid Response Teams

Promote the notion that Nexus Rapid Response Teams will be deployed to capture and contain members who commit grave harmful acts toward others. This includes those who lead others in similar harmful actions. Elitists have no special "powers" for tolerance regarding grave harmful acts. In short, all grave harmful acts will not be tolerated. There is no where to hide. Follow the harmful acts.

Nexus Peace Duty Caretakers

You have been selected to be members of our Nexus Rapid Response Teams because of your capacity to be peace-equalizing caretakers. You will develop in ways that will promote peace everywhere.

Pre-Adult and Adult Sponsor Caretakers

Sponsor Caretakers

This is a general classification whereby as sponsor caretakers of an entity, they will collectively participate in the caretaking decisions involving the entity. There will be no tolerance for selection determination confrontations. When primary determination confrontations ensue, those sponsor caretakers involved will be temporarily removed from sponsor caretaker status. Those sponsors remaining will be allowed to continue their responsibilities. With temporary sponsor removal status, those who show a sincere effort to be viable sponsor caretakers once again will be allowed back in the caretaking activities of an entity. Sponsor caretakers are to be viewed as providing the best form of caretaking.

Pre-Adult Sponsor Caretaker

Pre-adult members will have oversight sponsor caretakers to assist them in their adult-maturing development. The pre-adult sponsor caretakers are normally first assigned to parental entities unless relinquished by parents or when there is a high certainty that grave safety or grave developmental harm is imminent or has been done.

Those who are sponsor caretakers for a pre-adult will have the designation removed when harm is done or the potential for grave harm is imminent. No more than five primary or principal caretakers are assigned per pre-adult.

Until they reach or are declared adult-status entities, children who have serious issues pertaining to them are to be reviewed by the first pent-degree ascension prime. Prime of degree five is another name for the same designation. This is based on the parents/custodians who are their caretakers.

Default Ascension Prime Pre-Adult Oversight

Pent-degree ascension primes automatically oversee the care of pre-adults within the umbrella prime unless specific expanding degree ascension prime decisions override due to harmful environments that were not being addressed by the pent-degree ascension primes. This type of issue ought to be rare.

Five Year Term Minimum

Pre-adult caretakers will be specifically identified for five-year terms. Those who do participate in caretaker duties will normally be renewed.

Guardian Auspices

Pre-adult members (children) are automatically under the auspices of the first pent-degree pentarchy prime for matters pertaining to guardian oversights. No child will be invisible to this pent-degree pentarchy prime. It is one of their primary responsibilities in making this so. Reviews are made at this designation for identification and re-establishing of pre-adult sponsor caretaker designation. Recommendation for child-care events will be followed. Removal of designation is made when recent child endangerment events have been found to be true or imminent child endangerment is very probable and ever present.

Pre-Adult Support Payments

Dependent support when decreed will not be greater than what is given as universal dependent deduction purposes. The first pent-degree prime will make that determination. Even for entities of limited resources, amounts are the same and owed over time to ease the burden.

Automatic Sponsor Caretaker Assignments

Children will automatically have pre-adult sponsor caretakers assigned when natural adult family members are not available. These sponsor caretakers may not be perfect ones but will be ones who have the passion to do the best job they can. Only when serious harm is possible or has been done will the position be taken away. Sincere caretaking efforts are to be recognized and applauded.

Adult Designation

Bequeathing of an adult designation of an entity is made by the nexus pentarchy prime (in early pentarchy prime formation) or the first pent-degree pentarchy prime, whichever is closest to premiere foundation prime degree. This can be declared by an automatic age attainment directive or due to a prime determination request by an entity in question and subsequent opinion concurrence.

The nexus pentarchy prime will establish the maximum adult attainment age for all entities able to make effective sentient decisions of their own. The degree of effective sentient decision creation determination will be defined to encompass close to one hundred percent of members within the nexus prime.

Adult Sponsor Caretakers

When an adult entity is not able to respond because of medical or bodily impairment, those who have personal involvement will decide on the entity's behalf. When a dispute arises that challenges a right of sponsorship, the earliest degree umbrella pentarchy prime encompassing all parties will select the sponsor caretakers. If, however, a sponsor caretaker is determined to have a very minor involvement or none at all, the degree prime that initially review the matter can defer a decision to the degree minus-one foundation pentarchy prime encompassing the smaller member group.

When no adult sponsor caretakers are present, the premier foundation pentarchy prime is initially given the responsibility for the decision. When no adult sponsor caretaker is available and viable, the next ascension pentarchy prime will be responsible for the decision. This repeats until the pent-degree pentarchy prime is found. Load balancing spanning a greater degree than pent-degree umbrella prime may be needed on occasions when major catastrophic events do occur.

Only interested entities that were/are involved with the well being of another entity are to be the primary ones who have the particular entity's best interests in mind and spirit. An auspices instrument will not have ultimate decision over the welfare of the entity unless no sponsor caretakers have come forward with their declarations. Every effort will be made to have the entity's stay short.

Pentarchy Prime Governance

Leader Caretakers Umbrella Reach Oversight

Historically, a government based on a nation-state framework is based on the elite in positions as land-based lords. Wars were started to secure and maintain artificial boundaries or fences. Leader caretakers do not require borders to wisely lead the pool that selected them. They have umbrella reach oversight.

General Reach

Historically, the legal system defined and handled matters that pertain to properties and their holdings of them. Entities are not to be viewed as property but rather are to be viewed in the well being and protection of primes. It is up to wise leader caretakers to initiate when entities may pose a danger to other entities and their well being and protection.

Minimum of Two

Primes deal with matters involving two or more members in their respective primes. For matters involving a singular member, that singular member handles them. Respect for this autonomy is universal.

Premier Prime Directives

When no rules and regulations exist to address an issue by two or more members of an umbrella prime, then the responsibility for their creation is the domain of the leader caretakers of the umbrella prime. Initially, they may be general in scope and application. Time may be needed for wise refinements. The wise usage of "time" applies here.

Geographical and Environmental Domains

Geographical and environmental domains are preserved under the auspices of umbrella primes based on the "Rule of Five" described elsewhere. Exceptions for non-preservation and non-sustaining activities can only be considered when an ongoing plague is present or a real possibility. In this case, a greater degree prime may recognize the situation to be of grave concern and intercede for the well being of all.

Bequeathing Caretaking to the Next Degree

Jurisdiction occurs at the umbrella degree prime that effectively encompasses all parties in an issue. Bequeathing jurisdiction on a subject matter can be made to the next ascension degree for a period of five years.

Access to Information

There will be no restrictions on an entity's own information recorded anywhere. Access to domain information, which is maintained by any particular pentarchy prime, will be made available to all within the pentarchy prime umbrella. Those who administered treatments, for example doctors, will be governed by rules and guidelines that describe the information to be collected and stored.

Revenue Sharing

Any resources, historically referred to as "revenue" but is now used to refer to any resource, collected by ascension primes are to be shared by the umbrella foundation primes. The shared resources allocation is based on wise usage and need.

Environmental Stewardship

Leader caretakers will, after much consultation with advisory duty caretakers, identify land, sea, air, space zones, etc. that can be given temporary stewardship for business, foundation prime, and/or entity usage. All usage code standards for its use must be complied with for continuous privilege usage.

Professional Certification Boards

Establish monitoring and evaluation auspice boards for the professional duty caretakers. The auspices will provide performance qualification ratings to aid any entity's need for such information.

A Primary Mission Statement

A primary mission statement of pentarchy primes is the identification and promotion of caretakers in their wise caretaking of entities in their domains. Diversity exists and is universal. However, it would be advantageous to be uniform when common elements or application threads exist.

Final Decree

Leader caretakers are the final arbiters in all matters involving their umbrella primes, inclusive. As described elsewhere in this guidebook, rely on the Rule of Five for matters pertaining to usage of natural resources, businesses, and commerce regarding efficiencies and to prevent review and resolution matters from going to a halt. Auspices agencies are established to be instruments of pentarchy primes, where appropriate, to handle routine or common matters not pertaining to unique urgent consequence issues to the general umbrella primes. Our respective pentarchy prime leader caretakers will etch well-formed principles and guidelines to assist us in our pursuits.

Ownership of Information

Information produced or collected in a pentarchy prime is to be shared by all entities within its umbrella. The referenced pentarchy prime may be required to share it with other pentarchy primes at the same prime degree. Here is how it works. A foundation pentarchy prime can produce or collect information to be shared within its pentarchy prime umbrella. However, the next ascension pentarchy prime must decide to collect the same type of information before it can be shared with its umbrella primes. This constitutes the right to privacy and related matters.

Bequeathing Decision Review and Resolution Domain Review

Decisions are to be made at the earliest foundation degree prime whenever possible. Jurisdiction is to be respected and resolutions honored with no exception except as explicitly expressed elsewhere, because of the serious nature of the issue review item. Decisions can be delegated to the next ascension pentarchy prime when review and determination requests are made by the foundation prime. The resulting decision by the ascension prime with sufficient opinions by leader caretakers is then binding. A request for insight can also be requested. The opinion may be used in arriving at a decision for the foundation pentarchy prime decision. In both situations, a fee may be permissible. The criterion for a particular pentarchy prime to have responsibility for a decision is when an issue impacts two to five of the foundation pentarchy primes within the prime.

Collection Set of Information

Information collected within a pentarchy prime umbrella remains within it unless a prime directive by the umbrella prime is made releasing the information to the ascension prime. This rule does not apply when the ascension prime is also collecting similar information by all degree minus-one member primes.

Ascension Prime Serious Issue Review

It will be one of the primary missions for primes to uncover the truth in matters that are of the serious nature initiated by more foundation primes when matters are not brought to ascension primes for a variety of reasons. The final onerous is on applying wise usage of prime activity avenues.

Umbrella Prime Re-sizing

When entities from primes outside a particular umbrella prime have affected non-environment and commerce consortium actions by the more foundation degree umbrella prime and its members, then the umbrella prime is re-sized to encompass the greater spanning degree that is involved.

Pentarchy Prime Auspices Instruments and Practices

A Lease Arrangement

With pentarchy prime framework, there is no propensity for war over land as in historical frameworks. The need to guard boundaries is non-existent. Besides, what would you defend? Land is a caretaker lease arrangement with the umbrella primes affected. The wise usage of land is promoted by primes. Hoarding is not allowed.

The Service of Institutions

Pentarchy prime framework requires leader caretakers take charge and make wise decisions. Leader caretakers do not serve institutions. Institutions, hereafter known as Pentarchy Prime Instruments, exist when prime directives warrant them.

Auspices of Pentarchy Primes

Instruments responsible for rules and guidelines based on prime directives exist under the auspices of pentarchy primes.

Long Standing Instrument Organizations

The instrument organizations established by primes will certify professional ranks that are especially involved with the health, welfare, and security of its members. It is the responsibility of these same prime instrument organizations to review each certification on a periodic basis and when grave harm has been done or have a high degree of certainty of happening. The respective umbrella prime is liable for offenses when early warning signs were ignored.

Pentarchy Prime Instrument Review Period

The leader caretakers of a particular pentarchy prime have five days to void proposed standards and guidelines produced by auspices executive duty caretakers of the auspices prime instruments. Opinion review feedback by leader caretakers can assist in rapid refinements when proposals are voided. In general emergency and when decrees are not related, the time for rejection is twenty-five days. These auspices prime instruments are chartered with implementing guiding principles created by leader caretakers' prime directives.

Identification Access Speed Instrument

Every entity is a member of at most one premier foundation prime. All ascension primes are derived from foundation primes that every entity can eventually be identified. However, an identification access speed instrument can be used to greatly speed up admission or perform transactions to primes' societal activities. This can also be used to access information archived in auspice libraries.

Instruments Crafted

Instruments will be crafted to implement prime directives.

Items for Auspice Instruments

When auspice instruments are in place to handle prime directives implementation for uniformity and economy of scale, leader caretakers may choose to refer items for consideration to these auspice instruments. No additional opinion is needed or necessary.

Right Fit of Elements

When it pertains to instruments and resources, the right fit of these elements is used. There is no need to be stopped or delayed due to obsolete historical restricting views and obstacles.

Guiding Principles

All auspice instruments will have their rules and guidelines to include guiding principles placed in auspices library registers and archival instruments for all members of the umbrella primes to access.

Identification Instruments

As identification instruments are required by degree plus one umbrella prime directives, the foundation degree prime identification instruments can be used as verification.

Caretaker Constructs

In caretaker constructs, viable entities are held responsible and accountable for their actions and in-actions. We require that wise decisions be made and not the adherence to imaginary and artificial (man-made) law boundaries that varies over time by changing judicial discourse.

Goods and Services Requests

A guideline for an umbrella prime to consider is this. When a prime directive states an outcome or direction requiring goods and services, then a request for participation is sought. Consortiums that wish to participate will craft proposals detailing their involvement. The proposals are reviewed for fitness. Then up to five consortiums will be awarded contracts detailing their share of their participation.

Valid for 625 Days

When favorable environments exist, declarations of "marriage", as defined in historical references, are valid for 625 days. During that time, no new declarations of marriage can be made by the members involved. Choose your partner with care. Be caring as well.

Umbrella Money Instruments

An umbrella prime banking system, which is an umbrella prime consortium, uses umbrella money instruments based on the rule of five.

Special Prime Directive Instrument

Given a particular pentarchy prime, a leader caretaker can be selected by the degree prime to craft prime directive opinions and be automatically implemented for a specific class of review items requiring fast turnaround of decisions when harmful acts or urgent safety concerns are present. This form of special prime directive instrument is to be used in a time of great dynamic upheavals in our prime and environment domains.

Pentarchy Prime Issue Formation

Prime Directive

A prime directive is the outcome of issue review and discussion activities by a particular pentarchy prime. This is due to an issue involving matters that pertain to two or more of its members. The prime directive reflects on the issue and specifies the resolution regarding it.

Candidate Issues

Candidate issues for prime decisions are based on the high probability that interactions of entities exist.

Size the Issue

The size of an issue is reviewed first. Then the review and resultant opinion of the issue is made at the correct degree-size pentarchy prime based on the issue's reach.

No Issue Delays

A prime has five days to validate an issue involving two or more members are in fact within their respective umbrella prime jurisdiction. Otherwise, the next ascension prime is involved in the issue unless the ascension prime cannot validate within five days. This process continues until an umbrella prime is found. This rule illustrates the importance of prime members' record keeping caretaking and preservation.

Types of Issues

Primarily, leader caretakers will be involved with types of issues that have not been addressed before. Established prime directives that are in existence at the present will govern normal or routine issues.

Matters brought to the Fore

Pentarchy primes deals with matters not specified anywhere else as rules and guidelines that were implemented or previously defined prime directives.

New Issues

All existing prime directives must be in compliance before new issues raised by a prime member can be considered and handled by the prime's leader caretakers. To be in compliance can mean a scheduled action as set forth by prime directive(s). Exceptions are when matters pertain to grave harm that has been committed or there is a high degree of certainty that grave harm will be committed by the member. Exceptions are also grave emergencies due to nature or other sentients with no malice for grave harmful acts.

Towards Ascension Prime

By registering your prime directives, future resolution petitions will more effectively review available information in rendering a newly created wise prime directive. These early directives set the stage for future directives at all degrees. All opinions do count.

Pentarchy Prime Issue Resolution

Initial Pentarchy Prime Issue Requester

When a prime decision has been made and passed on to members within the prime who had the issue initially presented to the prime then the members must abide by it. Failure to comply by any member will cause suspension of further consideration for any current and future issue review requests brought by the non-compliant member.

Interim Consuls

We will have interim consuls and arbiters to handle the transitional judicial reviews. Prime tenets are supreme and the consuls and arbiters will ensure that these tenets are not violated when reviewing historical references.

Leader Caretaker Opinions

For any prime, three yes opinions are needed for a decision to have creditable prime directive status recognition. In time of emergencies, one leader caretaker of the five in a prime is needed for a temporary decision to be carried out. Within 25 hours, the complement of the three minimum decisions is needed to remove a temporary decision to be longer term. Contingencies may need to be considered, which is why these temporary measures are needed. These events ought to be rare.

Text Available to All

The text to all prime decisions will be made available to all entities within the umbrella prime. The exceptions will be when there is a high probability that should a decision be made readily available, there is a high degree of certainty that grave harmful acts may be committed by those who are viewed as violent entities and are not presently in confinement.

Record Keeping

An information system will be developed and maintained to keep track of all associations. Access to it is to be easily acquired by any member within the umbrella prime. Any matter involving two or more pentarchy primes at the same prime degree will be resolved by the immediate ascension pentarchy prime encompassing all. A pentarchy prime session will convene as needed.

Source of Resolution Insights

Reviewing member foundation primes' prime directives by umbrella prime members does provide good insights regarding the health and wise decision making activities of the more foundation primes. Umbrella prime can determine when assistance is urgently needed.

The Rule of Five Review and Resolution Ceiling

On occasions, there may be appeals to the next ascension prime to determine if a particular prime directive is viewed as harsh for the requester. If so, a review is stated with comment and passed to foundation prime or petitioner requesting this review. A refinement prime directive may be crafted. This process repeats until five degrees of ascension primes from the reference prime have been contacted. Review and resolution can yield a neutral outcome. It this case, the original prime directive is left as-is.

Interim Directives

Some issues can be deferred when the subject matter requires more thought and discovery. In those cases, an interim directive will be issued and have a preface stating that this directive is interim in scope and that the issue may be re-visited at a later time after additional thought and discovery activities.

Progress Reports

Provision for Confinement in Error

Since there is always a chance that an entity may be confined in error, once a new review followed by a new hearing has been conducted because significant new information and validations are uncovered, release is immediate, in less than twenty-five hours.

Reel Them In

For egos that are too pronounced, it may be wise to reel them in by selecting their successors.

Prime Auspice Libraries

Dedication

This is dedicated to those sentients who recognized the importance for the archival and retrieval of the word by the wisest leader caretakers closest to All-That-Is.

It is an Honor

Library Motto: "It is an honor and of prime importance to be of service".

Role of Pentarchy Prime Library

Pentarchy prime libraries are instruments that provide very long term archival and retrieval of prime directive services plus offer a very high degree of reliability as to their references. They are the prime concerns and pursuits provided that the time and resources are not prohibited. This includes the instruments used by auspice scribes to record prime directives and recognized events.

Characteristic Elements of Auspice Library

There is no single historical reference that closely identifies with an Auspices Library. One may find numerous elements from many different historical references. However, not all the characteristic elements can be found.

Recording System Centers (RSC)

Prime directives or determinations will be sent to Recording System Centers (RSC) described elsewhere. These RSC will identify all entities affected by the decisions and send copies to them. For more serious violations, rapid deployment teams in close proximity to entity or entities will deliver the copies.

The primes will fund an independent service organization that is chartered to record all new or changed entity premiere foundation prime information and all prime directives. Universal entity and prime directive identifiers will be used to identify the records for easy archival and retrieval. The accuracy is to be viewed as of the highest importance possible.

Designated Establishment

Auspice library instrument access is at designated umbrella prime establishments found strategically throughout.

Meeting Center and Access Routes

The prime auspices library will determine prime meeting center address and access routes. Of prime consideration is to be accessible to close to one hundred percent of the members of the associated ascension prime that it is charted to.

Access to Auspices Library

Access to an auspices library is primarily for members of the umbrella pentarchy prime that charted it.

Auspice Library Characteristics

1. Neutral Instrument
2. No enforcement doctrine
3. Rapid recording instrument
4. Rapid retrieval instrument
5. Message instrument

A Messaging System

Auspice Library maintains a messaging system with the following partial list of features.

1. Notification regarding prime directives to members of the umbrella prime who are impacted by them.
2. Notification regarding requests for opinions and remedies on habitual or defiant non-compliance by members to the degree plus one umbrella prime.

Message Caretakers

Auspice libraries are chartered with prime directive registries and any other registries stated in prime directives. Implementation of them is excluded from auspice library activities. Their primary focus is one of being the message caretakers of pentarchy prime activities.

Prime Directive Registry Entries

Build automatic auspices library entry instruments to register newly created Prime Directives. However, they are not certified until proper authentication procedures and declarations are made by at least three leader caretakers of a particular prime. The need to automate provides other degree primes with early prime directive information to assist in their own discovery and resolution activities. However, any final reference to other prime directives must be official ones.

Archival Prime Directive Identification

An important role of the auspices library is the registry and archival of prime directives with unique archival prime directive identifications assigned to them for rapid retrieval when requested.

Delay Responses

It is of prime importance to minimize delay responses for prime directive retrieval requests. Leader caretakers require all available information so that more effective prime directives can be crafted for matters of prime importance and at the earliest possible moment.

Record Keeping Charter

Record keeping systems, such as a conceptually recognized computer systems complete with backup and disaster recovery procedures or other similar permanent recording and safeguarding instruments, will record entity foundation prime selection. There is a universally recognized tenet that puts a restriction for an entity to be active in only one premiere foundation pentarchy prime. This is one of the many purposes for the set of instruments known simply as Prime Auspices Libraries.

Pent-Degree Ascension Prime Record Keeping

At each multiple pent-degree ascension prime designation starting with the first, record-keeping systems will be established and maintained within each of these pent-degree umbrella primes. The nexus prime will also maintain a nexus system even when not at a pent-degree. The information is collected starting with the nearest pent-degree ascension prime designation from nexus prime record keeping system. Each pent-degree ascension prime record keeping system will do the same until the foundation primes are reached. It is to archive only prime directives and declarations crafted at a particular pent-degree minus one to the pent-degree.

Record keeping of individual prime directives will be maintained by the respective prime. It is a requirement to also archive prime directives to the nearest ascension pent-degree Prime Directive Library. This is important when ascension prime directive creation uses compliance determination to arrive at the final decree. However, the research information collection set that formed the basis for the prime directive is not required for archival with the respective prime directive. This affords confidentiality of the information used in the crafting of the prime directives.

Alternate sites to be use as backup archives would be wise to have. Only when an ascension prime directive requires the same information regarding its umbrella foundation primes for the purpose of arriving at a decision at the ascension prime will the ascension prime retain a copy of the information.

Standard Instruments and Procedures

Standard instruments (forms) and procedures are to be crafted and used wherever possible for effective archiving and retrieval of prime directives. Supporting attachments can also be tagged as artifact and archived for later retrieval using standard instruments (forms) and procedures.

Standard Fees

Standard fees will be established and revised as needed for the purpose of assessment for registering prime directives into archival registries. For those who cannot immediately handle the fees, the amount will be added to their prime account, which must be paid eventually by the prime or an ascension prime.

Resource Funding

Registry copies of any prime directive may be given to members for a fee when deemed needed to help out in the operational costs for particular Pentarchy Prime Auspice Libraries.

Types of Prime Registries

Prime Registries for:
1. Members Marriage Declarations
2. Member Births
3. Member Expirations
4. Foundation Prime Births
5. Foundation Prime Expirations
6. Ascension Degree Prime Births
7. Ascension Degree Prime Expirations
8. Nexus Prime Designation Updates
9. Registration of all new members that join.
10. Registration when there is the suspension of professional duties for a member in a degree prime and the member joins another degree prime. Access to prime directives for the suspension is granted in determining whether the member (entity) can resume professional duties in the newly joined degree prime.
11. More items to be filled here as needed.

False Registries

Charge backs will be made to degree minus-one umbrella primes toward the foundation primes that intentionally put forth false registries, such as, intentional false reports of missing persons, violent acts, prime directives that cannot be certified, etc. In this way, every degree prime towards the actual degree prime that put forth the original false registries will be aware of this. Then discoveries and remedies will be made to reduce these false registries to zero. Truth and information integrity is paramount for a healthy prime.

Automatic Registry of Marriage

Auspice library's automatic registry of marriages (family bonds) declarations is initiated by the parties themselves. No one can do this on any parties' behalf. They must register at the auspice library spanning the parties. Should visits by auspice duty caretaker be necessary due to the parties' reduced mobility capabilities, these visits are permitted and advised.

Special Event Recordings

Recordings of actual events will be kept for safe keeping by the qualifying ascension prime satisfying the Rule of Five prime determination test based on the members participating or as spectators in the event.

Urgent Archive of Prime Directives

It is an urgent matter to record and archive prime directives in the manner described elsewhere even in those happenings when action results will not be forthcoming in the near future due to forced compliance by pre-pentarchy prime systems. When the event occurs that highlights the eminence of pentarchy prime supremacy, all prime directives are activated, if not already. Those who willfully interfere with pentarchy prime directives and activities will be subject to privilege limiting directives depending on the severity of the interference.

Lifeline of Sentient Health

Access to auspices libraries are not normally denied to a member of the respective umbrella primes. Auspices duty caretakers will turn around prime directive searches in the most expeditious manner when possible. Auspices duty caretakers who loose the passion to serve will have their stay declared with an expiration date. It is of prime importance that prime directive retrievals are performed with reasonable speed. Our prime leader caretakers depend on this service so that their subsequent wise prime directive creations can be speedy as well using all available information. The umbrella primes depend on this need. In other words, you also depend on this lifeline of sentient health.

Sustenance

Auspice library archival and retrieval are the key factors for effective prime directive creations and implementation. One might call it sustenance for a vibrant umbrella environment.

Non-Implementation Language Initially

Archive prime directives in every situation even when no implementation language is included. Time will ensure that all prime directives are complied with through refinement of the language. Wait and see.

Terminology Archived

The terminology defined or referenced in this book is archived for later retrieval by the duty caretakers of the prime auspice libraries.

Follow-up Reports

Follow-up reports will be produced using aspice libraries for the respective umbrella primes as the distributors of information in these umbrella primes.

Keystone

The auspice library is the keystone to effective pentarchy prime resolutions because of its charter to archive and retrieve all prime directives. Prime directives that span historical "political" domains may have appeared not to be enforceable in the beginning. However, they did alert members of the umbrella primes that are spanning these domains to take action in removing all of the "officials" that were in violation.

Early-Informed Duty Caretakers

Auspice library duty caretakers provide notifications of prime directives to members that have been impacted by them. Notifications are also made when prime directives have expired. The onus will not entirely rests on members to find out. Auspice library duty caretakers are in a better position because of being the early-informed ones when events happen.

A Walk Through Historical Time

When one has been selected to be a duty caretaker for an auspice library, then she will discover that the auspice library provides a most favorable environment in which to walk through historical time to the present and be awed by the achievements made by sentients. As one researches the archival of prime directives, the path that a particular pentarchy prime took did not occur by happenstance. Rather, they occur by the desires and passions of sentients for attaining a higher level of awareness and spiritual development.

Wisely Crafted Prime Directives

I will know you by your wisely crafted prime directives. They become the windows into the intimate insights into who and what you are.

Wiser and Wiser in Perpetuity

Pentarchy prime's auspice library is the key to crafting wiser and wiser prime directives in perpetuity with unimpeded access to its archive.

Moment Passages

Auspice library is a great place to grasp the essence of being sentient. The prime directives that one will have ready access to can be reviewed and studied. These activities can bring one to the lead up and moment of the actual moment passages. Hence, the prime directives are found to be timeless.

Prime Auspices Library Duty Caretakers

It is an Honor to Serve

It is an honor to serve an Auspices Library. As a benefit, the Auspices Library provides a great learning experience into the vitality of an umbrella prime.

To Recent Arrivals

The Auspice Library duty caretakers who have joined will rapidly discover a universal view and gain intimate insights in the harmonious at-one-ment with the Nexus. It is a realm that is alive and not that of museums.

Stay a While

You are embarking on an honorable vocation as an auspices library caretaker. The establishment of a pentarchy prime instrument to efficiently store and retrieve prime directives will result in the construct of a pillar foundation for effective prime activities. It is an extreme honor to serve a noble position such as this. As an auspices caretaker, one must put aside leanings towards a position of being for or against particular prime directives. The total recall of any and all prime directives is instrumental in the vibrant and health of pentarchy primes. Should you choose otherwise, there is no disgrace in pronouncing your orderly intentions of relinquishing your active role as a caretaker. However, the longer your stay is, your umbrella prime will greatly appreciate it. It is with sincere hope that your stay is a learning experience in your pursuits in serving the degrees of primes that you wish to serve. Consider being a mentor to others. Best wishes.

Transitional Challenges towards Pentarchy Prime

A Mirror Reflection

There are times when laws are passed so that officials and non-officials can commit criminal acts as viewed by some but not violate any of these laws. However in all cases, natural laws still prevail. This notion is hidden from those who are "law abiding". A mirror reflection will occur in time.

Feudal Terrorists

By peacefully assembling to proclaim your prime directives to land (feudal) lords, you will learn who the true terrorists are.

Shout the Loudest

Those who shout the loudest for "justice" and the "rule of law" are the ones who are the power recipients of the current belief system. Their affiliation has been exposed by their actions.

Disparate Systems

Why have disparate historical systems? Choose umbrella primes.

Pre-Prime Phase

For those who rely on primitive resolution systems, this suggests that these entities are at a pre-prime maturity developmental phase. No viable sentient agreements can be crafted with them.

Governance Oversight for All

Just as in nature, sentients in corporeal form will sense that something has gone awry to a great degree. The result of this in historical times is civil war to purge those who have abused their positions of governance oversight for all. With primes, the needs of the umbrella are addressed since everyone has a voice to the selection of leader caretakers. Issues are "right-sized" and reviewed by the proper degree prime effectively spanning all involved in the respective issue.

Submission to Reign of Terror

Why not construct a framework whereby wise decisions are promoted. Choose to participate in the selection of your leader caretakers. Their decision crafting are not based in a feudal system framework, which has references of barbarous times, but are based on what is truly needed in the here and now. To wait for the judicial system to catch up with urgent matters is to submit to the reign of terror by the few who preside over their subjects. Choose to have leader caretakers decide based on sizing the matter and sizing the degree prime that will review and opinion crafted.

Spans the World

In recent historical references, some would say that the Greatest Society's Justice System was declared to be the fairest in the world. This is not so. The vast majority of the world's population could not participate. Upon reflection, is this fair? With the Pentarchy Prime framework, everyone is a participant and has an influence in the selection of leader caretakers. This feature spans the world.

In Perpetuity

To continue down repeating historical paths will result in wars and atrocities in perpetuity.

Barbarous System Artifacts

In recent historical times, we supported backward leaning judicial systems. The promotion of society's well being is not the aim when legal opinions are foremost in their charter. Commonly, finding fault and punishment is. What barbarous system artifacts they are, which may still be in use today. Is it clearer to you now? The decisions of the few override the decisions of the many. When we decide to fix an expiration date for this type of institutional relic and take wise caretaking activities seriously will the world be a peaceful and tranquil satellite revolving around the warmth and glow of the sun.

Executions are Banned

If the nation-state wants to set an example for the premise that no harmful acts will be promoted, then it must begin by not executing anyone in captivity. There are no exceptions. Executions of any kind are banned, or so it is proclaimed.

Spanned Transitional Government Domains

During the transitional period, transitional spanned government domains that effectively mirror the umbrella prime that they span will form an interim consortium presided by the leader caretakers of the particular umbrella prime that spans them. All cooperative directives will be complied by the instruments of the consortium.

Wise Doctrine

A wise doctrine is one that declares that no embargo will be used on a "nation-state" to the detriment of the captured citizens who are viewed as properties of the nation-state. A wise doctrine is to allow safe passage for sentients everywhere.

Twenty-Five Year Renewal

During the transitional period, any law that is to be kept requires a political or legislative proponent or sponsor who has declared her passion for its passage and implementation. However, a twenty-five year renewal passage must subsequently be made for the law to not automatically expire.

Viewed as Perfect

There are those who believe that their historical systems are sound because of their need to arrive at decisions that are as perfect as possible whereby the application of their decisions can be applied to each and every feudal subject equally. The fallacy is that subjects are to be viewed as perfect. This fallacy is why historical systems implode based on the decisions of the few. We are not homogenized entities, which is why societal systems need to adjust to encompass diversity in their membership pools. Members are not identical in responses and awareness. Learning setbacks will be experienced. Yearning to advance is innate in all of us when we listen to ourselves. Allow groups to work out challenges for themselves on condition that their activities do not violate basic tenets for the entire umbrella pool. These tenets ensure that every member can be viable entities.

Urgent Need to Balance Out

You will find that as the pentarchy prime framework takes hold, there will be a very large number of prime directive creations due to the urgent need to balance out the cruel historical systems that promoted violent outcomes at all costs. This will happen even when the beliefs by members for these historical systems wane.

Automaton Mold

To be all things to all people become a bottleneck. Consider not relying on fitting a single universal automaton mold. We can be more effective.

Property Value

A level playing field for child support will be set during the transitional period to pentarchy prime framework. The financial and caretaking support is fair and equitable for every child. No child will be viewed as having more "property value" than another child has because of the level of wealth holdings of the parents.

All-Inclusive

The members of the elite are in positions of oversight until their beliefs in the system wavers and a vote of no confidence results. Dare to choose an all-inclusive surroundings.

Accurate Reporting

As part of the entourage of auspices prime caretakers, a recording crew will accompany those who are being recorded and filmed by non-pentarchy prime members during the transitional period. This is to ensure that accurate reporting can be validated by non-pentarchy prime framework construct. We are not fooled.

Transitional Cooperatives

Use of pentarchy prime cooperatives, such as credit unions by non-members, is not allowed during the transitional period.

Invalid

To pass laws regarding non-citizens and external nation-state governments is invalid. Without the umbrella span to include all sentients, the "greatness" of these "civilized nation-states" is in actuality, not so. Exclusions make their great framework hollow and without form.

Consider Diversity of Beliefs

Are you aware that members will actually die and/or kill for their strongly held beliefs? How about we consider this. Permit members to retain their diversity of beliefs as long as the beliefs are not imposed on one another. The umbrella prime framework makes this so.

We are a Living Society

We are a living society. We require living caretakers to take charge of crafting wise decisions. Artificial constructs constructed long ago have little relevance regarding important matters of today. In order for us to develop even more, we require that we be in charge and not the antiquated framework of the elite.

Free to Choose

An argument will surface that the status quo is sufficient and enduring. The status quo claims that we are all free to choose. Then those who believe in this argument ought not to be fearful with a pentarchy prime framework when the argument's premise is that everyone is free to choose. Then allow us to choose our own framework.

Early Pentarchy Prime Directive

Historical state constructs will be directed to stop all their terrorist practices.

Central Controls

In recent historical times, we are blocked from making and implementing wise decisions by artificial central controls. We are now decentralized. It is much easier this way.

Instrument of Designation

Every foundation pentarchy prime member will authenticate an instrument of designation that records and archives its members' pronounced agreements called prime directives, which are supreme to all other non-prime directives during transitional periods. Non-compliance will result in immediate revocation of membership and future remedies. Any reinstatement requires long and arduous reinstatement activities. The selection of a foundation pentarchy prime will be made on their behalf with the privilege of being selected to the next degree prime suspended for a period of time defined by the first pent-degree pentarchy prime for the foundation prime. This will normally be defined as five years once the pentarchy prime framework has been established for a period of twenty-five years.

Set of Incremental Prime Directives

Do not challenge non-prime framework in their arenas unless the umbrella primes lead by our leader caretakers span the particular arenas. When this happens, then the issuing of prime directives spelling out the actions that will be taken by the umbrella prime will be crafted. For members failing to comply with prime directives regarding non-prime frameworks will be identified and have their prime privileges suspended to include issue reviews initiated by them. For example, failure to vote in a non-prime framework election event in selecting candidates identified as prime selections will have one or more of the member's prime privileges suspended. The sequence of the set of prime directives pertaining to non-prime frameworks is incremental and crafted over time. In this way, the damaging impacts to prime members are minimized.

A Tranquil Environment Thrives

You will find that when a greater number of members participate in decision generating prime directives, then a more tranquil environment thrives. This eventuality will eclipse the few decision-makers whose tenacity forces us to be slaves to these few elite. Choose for yourself.

Sum of Its Parts

An umbrella prime comprised of degree minus-one primes within the umbrella is greater than the sum of its parts. Likewise, the melding of historical "nation-states" eliminates the notion of feudal (land based) wars. With a prime framework, no borders exist to fight over. It would be feudal to do so.

Transitional Library Associations

The establishment of a Library of Prime Directives will occur that will have no association with any other organization to include direct association to pentarchy primes while the prevailing historical governance frameworks are non-pentarchy prime frameworks.

To Grasp Terrorism

Fabricated states think that they have a monopoly on terms such as terrorism whereby they can exclude themselves in this category. They seem to think that their form of terrorism is legitimate. In the realm of ATI, their true nature is known for entities to grasp. However, an entity must be receptive in using those abilities that will help her gain the insights that are in her reach.

Requirement Based Access

When there is a requirement, such as medical shots, the collective caretaker instrument must provide for it when members do not have the means or access to have it done.

Reinforced by the State

Due to the condemnation of self, which was reinforced by the state, no support is provided by the state. Rather, passive and, at times, obvious resistance is provided instead. Bypass their limited assistance and address self directly to the societal pool. You will find that pentarchy primes, on the other hand, are based on statements of freedom and spiritual power.

State Required Experts for Everyone

For some, there is the notion that insists that experts are the only ones who can handle particular matters. If that is the case, then the experts must handle all member concerns. For example, if doctors are the only ones who can handle medical care, then the state must guarantee that the doctors are available to everyone. There is no exception. Since this is not the case, courts cannot rule against any guardian who does not have access to these expert doctors because, for instance, the guardian has no funds to pay for them.

Concrete Institutions

When Earth makes corrections, the concrete institutions of the world will crumble.

Based on Available Information

Give non-prime officials a chance to meet with leader caretakers to answer questions. Failure to meet will lead to crafting prime directives based on available information and not on any information that these officials may have. They will find that it would be advantageous to be forthcoming with the information that is requested. These refusals will be recorded for later dispositions regarding non-compliant officials.

The Best Interest of the Child Test

The best interest of the child promotes a class society. Those without adequate support are not given the same minimum sustenance as those of greater support. Therefore, this test fails to adequately promote the equitable support of sustenance to every child.

For Expediency Sake

Some "experts" are not very good at what they do. For them, actions and decisions are made for expediency sake. Be aware of these types of expert advice. Above all, choose wisely.

Transitional Taxes

No real estate taxes are recognized since no member "owns" real estate. It is a lease arrangement with the umbrella prime spanning affected members. Real estate is an historical referential construct. Real-time goods and services activities can be taxed for pentarchy prime revenues used for auspices instrument operations until a superior monetary instrument is crafted. Vibrant interactions are promoted in this manner and not the hoarding of real estate.

A Greater Vision

Great societies do not need military night vision instruments to have a greater vision in darkness. See the things for what they are in daylight. The military apparatus is not required for a greater vision.

Separate and Distinct

Consider primes. Only in this way will your directives be known. By subscribing to a belief system that requires "individuals" to be viewed solely as "separate and distinct", this affords the elite the ability to divide and conquer the masses. The individual is then an army of one, which is easier to defeat.

Nature has a way of showing anyone who chooses to see that separate individuals make up a whole. Consider conjoined twins. How is this possible? This question is asked whenever we find this in nature. The perspective is really that it is possible. Consider the possibilities!

A Net Placed Over Harmful Acts

On another matter regarding historical references, cruel and violent acts are viewed with the same adversarial arena with sentences and not guilty verdicts whereby violent actors can be set free due to legal maneuvering. In a pentarchy prime framework, a high degree of certainty is not needed when the safety of members is the chief concern in the beginning. Retaining members that may be the actors regarding the grave harmful acts will allow a net large enough to, in all likely-hood, catch the offending actors. As more information is discovered, the high degree of certainty regarding the offenders will be forthcoming. The retention of an artifact system complete with dungeons historically called jails is not supported.

In the Best Interest of the Child - Custodial Parent

Consider "in the best interest of the child", which is a recent historical guideline in a feudal system. The custodial parent is not representative of the general population. A woman will have physical custody in more than 90 percent of the time. The child is still viewed as property of the woman. Exclusion of a large percentage of the population in the caretaking activities still prevails in this view. The feudal system disregards the caretaking interests of other members in its pool. Property rights are enforced no matter what the outcome. To do otherwise will cause this system to implode because its primary foundation tenet is obliterated.

Deter and Punish

There exist in historical terms the notion that jail sentencing is the best way to "deter and punish" those who commit degrees of "felony" classification of violations. This is simply not the case. Removing privileges in day-to-day experiences for violators is best and can be tailored to the violation. The historical "all or nothing" approaches do in fact promote condemning institutions and industries in perpetuity. In the pentarchy prime framework, severe or repeated acts will result in confinement in camps or high security prime protection facilities.

Executors of Non Prime Directive Orders

The following concerns the transitional period to pentarchy prime framework pertaining to Pentarchy Prime Auspice Libraries. When non prime members in historical frameworks execute orders issued by historical courts or through official papers by agencies affecting pentarchy prime members will have automatic prime directive registry entries made for each non-prime member that executed the orders. These non-prime members are registered in Pentarchy Prime Auspice Library archives stating their violations of confidentiality whereby future issues for review involving them will have degrees of magnitude stipulations of non-compliant remedies be required for fulfillment before any future prime directives involving them can be crafted and implemented. This is due in whole or in part on their earlier violations. Recording of violations is automatic. The crafting of prime directives encompassing them is done in the future.

The Practice of Distroying

There is a dilemma by some of our historical duty caretakers in raising great numbers of livestock only to be "destroyed" instead of raising them and later butchered because of widespread diseases in the livestock. A better approach is to examine whether the practice of appropriate caretaking is being performed. The practice of "destroying of livestock" reflects poorly on our humane ways of livestock caretaking. All of us suffer negatively. The pain and sorrow are manifested in society in ways that may appear to be not related to the actual events. The more pronounced manifestation may appear as unexplained erratic and irrational behaviors by members in society. Those who are sensitive to the cause and effect are aware of these connections. ATI, please forgive us for we do not know what we have done.

Diversity of Life Habitats

There are those who believe that allowing everyone to pass within each other's border will turn the landscapes to a sea of camps. In the short term, some of these landscapes will occur as sentients adjust to freedom of movement. In the long term, pentarchy primes will settle into ones where members can best identify with. The best fit for members will offer them the most promise, which does not necessarily mean relying on established institutions or geographical areas. Diversity of life habitats will seed and flourish instead. The scenery will be one of beauty and tranquillity.

Chartered for Wisdom

Historical judicial systems are not chartered to make wise decision, only legal ones. We require wise leader caretakers to craft and render wise prime directives and opinions. Pentarchy primes are viewed to promote just that since members will participate in the selection of the leader caretakers to the next degree primes. The pentarchy prime framework is charted for wisdom all the way to the nexus.

Travel Instruments

Historical World Body, such as the United Nations of the Twentieth Century, Travel Instruments can be used anywhere in the world with no detention or delays when no World Body (United Nations) violations have been made.

Neutral Ground

The recent historical reference "world body" framework known as the United Nations, in order to foster an even playing field, needs to relocate to a neutral location not belonging to any member's nation-state boundary so that more effective decisions can be made during the transitional time towards pentarchy primes. The location will be complete with necessary infrastructures to include access routes and diverse means of transportation. In this way, discussions and decision outcomes can truly be on neutral ground.

Corporations are Not Sentient

Corporations as defined in historical references are not superior to sentients. A corporation is not a sentient entity. Laws describing rules and guidelines during the transitional period towards pentarchy primes will be directed to sentients who managed and run them. Adaptation to consortiums is the long-term perspective.

The Condemning Industry

The condemning industry spans all other types of industries. It permeates in everything in society. One might say that it is a cancer with no chance of a cure. All will suffer. Let us reverse the cancerous growth and expire the industry. We are not viably served by it. This industry does not promote peace and tranquillity.

Going Bankrupt

We have to get out of the condemning business or go bankrupt.

They Wait for No One

To wait for a judicial session in historical references after a long period of time has elapsed after grave harmful activity events serves neither justice nor the people that the judicial system is supposedly protecting. Leader caretakers in a pentarchy prime framework, on the other hand, are astutely adept at crafting prime directives in a timely manner. They wait for no one in rendering wise decisions.

Renegade Nation in Check

The recent historical framework called the United Nations cannot long endure when even one renegade member nation exists among them. The renegade must be kept in check.

Assets Depleted

When assets of historical frameworks are depleted, that's when pentarchy primes will take hold.

The "Best Interest" Test Excludes

In the "best interest of the child" test, it does not apply to the unborn. Exclusion is being applied here too. The promotion of inclusion is a basic premise of pentarchy prime.

Education and Awareness Activities

Part of the caretaker organizational instruments' (COI) purpose is the education and awareness activities for COI rules and regulations by participating members. For example, members affected by vehicle use and licensing.

Prime Qualified Candidate

When elections for an official in historical terms and there is no candidate that is prime-qualified before the ballots for the election are finalized, write-ins may be done at election time for a prime-qualified candidate.

Same Duration In or Out

However long it took one to get into a situation may take just as long to get out.

Wise Indeed

Historical experts are unable to render wise decisions since their "expert advice (conclusion)" is dependent on their own personal "school of thought". Wise leader caretakers will rely on the entire set of insights. They are wise indeed!

Care Choices

When we choose to care in total, artificial constructs will not long endure (stand much longer). We will then be free of obstacles in the caring of all. We are then free to choose one of many care choices.

Laws Terminated

We do not promote the practice of breaking of laws. We promote the dismantling of sentient inhibiting laws through the termination process. Then these laws cannot be broken when they are terminated. Why would we want to keep some laws active when they inhibit sentient pursuits?

Holy Books

If tradition requires that one place one's hand on a bible to take an oath of office, the bible will not be just one particular version. They will be all of the spiritual references representing the pentarchy prime umbrella based, at a minimum, on the rule of five.

Diversity in Transportation Routes and Constructions

Diversity in transportation routes and constructions are essential to sentients vitality. Separate transportation for what is historically referred to as "military means" will be minimal. Personnel will use public domain systems without being charged the fare. A tally may be kept for utilization analysis. Straddling in the use of them is the norm. These peace caretakers will blend in the pool's community. No distinctive advantage will be provided. In this way, these diverse transportation means can combine both "public" and "private" monies to construct and maintain wonderful transportation marvels. A requirement that peace duty caretakers be in uniform is required so that no fees are assessed at the time of boarding. Undercover peace duty caretaker will need to pay fees unless identification instruments denoting their duty status can be produced.

The Property of Children

We must stop promoting the notion that children are property. I for one am not a slave owner.

Shaped into Submission and Transformed

There is an observation that we have been shaped into submission to an autocratic framework. To transform into a sentient framework will require participation in deriving prime directives. It starts with the word set into motion by having it spoken.

Timing of Prime Directives

When a prime directive spanning non-prime systems as described elsewhere is ignored, honoring prior-prime system frameworks made after the prime directive event will not be recognized or considered when prime framework is universally implemented spanning these non-prime systems. New determinations will be required. However, the playing field will be different. The resulting prime directives will most likely follow different outcomes. Those who violate prime directives when they were made aware of them will go through a process of evaluation to determine fitness in the positions that they currently hold. These guidelines and rules are covered in greater detail elsewhere.

World Bodies

Recent historical references of world bodies, for example the United Nations, are auspices instruments should a umbrella prime decides to continue to use them. This will be based on the particular world body's performance and efficiencies.

The "Law of Exclusion"

In historical frameworks, those who are identified as non-citizens and who are not in confinement are still not permitted to vote in a particular societal pool. This is the "law of exclusion". Only those who are in confined for grave harmful acts that have been committed or that have been prevented to a high degree of certainty by Nexus Rapid Response Teams or Nexus auspice instruments will not be permitted to participate. The Nexus pentarchy prime has ultimate responsibilities in matters regarding grave harmful acts and resolutions.

Obsolete Judicial Cartel

Judicial cartel is not practiced in pentarchy prime framework. It is obsolete.

Held to the Same Ideals

In order to make this work, everyone will have to denounce executions or grave harmful acts of any kind. This includes anyone in captivity. We will be held to the same ideals that we expect others to have. In summary, there will be no executions of any kind.

Handling Interference Events

Auspice library duty caretakers will not be put in severe event outcomes by non-prime courts or official agencies. They will, however, automatically record these interference events. They will follow guidelines crafted by umbrella prime leader caretakers that span these non-prime institutions regarding the notifications and automatic infraction recordings. These violations will be viewed as severe requiring action plans and their implementation for their quick removal and expiration of these officials and institutions.

Transitional Court Systems

The historical basic concept of "court systems" can be used in prime framework during the transitional period. These systems will be specialize to render auspice specific interpretations to rules and guidelines crafted and maintained by their respective auspice umbrella prime. These evolved systems will be discovered to offer uniformity and economy of scale. Duplicity of overlapping systems will be diminished to zero in time. It is universally recognized, though, that the umbrella prime a particular auspice court system is chartered to has supreme interpretations by its leader caretakers. This will occur on those rare occasions when clarity of interpretation is wisely concluded. Hence, this option exercised by leader caretakers is to be used when needed.

Rogue Nation-States

In historical references, we have a world body chartered with the formation of world policies and guidelines. Its charter ought to include keeping all rogue nation-states in check. Make it so.

Relying on Laws

We are tripping over ourselves in relying on laws to do the right thing. Laws do not promote wise decisions, sentients do. Allow leader caretakers, who are not made of laws, to be the final arbiters. After all, we have selected them to perform just that.

Hope is on Its Way

It is a good thing when a potential grave harmful act has been dwarfed and stopped. The confinement will not, however, be greater than the minimum for the extinguishing act of a member by another. The kind act of prevention changed the potential grave harmful act into one of peace and hope. Consider being a peace caretaker. Then there is a greater chance for hope to be on its way.

System Continuance

Judicial systems can only exist as auspices of pentarchy prime umbrellas via prime directives when determined that their continuance can be effective and efficient in handling economy of scale results.

Transitional Emergency Response Team

A number of pentarchy prime books have been written to provide early awareness of things to come when feudal systems rapidly implode and become non-viable in order to advance all of society. Those who practice pentarchy prime framework early on will have the easiest time during these transformational times towards sentient awareness. I salute you for your insightful preparations. You become part of the transitional emergency response team to bring about a peaceful and tranquil environment.

Playing Field

Business is business. However, pentarchy primes will define the playing field arena for all that desire to be a part of it.

Evolutionary Nature of Things

A replacement framework is in the works. This will replace all the historical ones, which greatly hampers the evolutionary nature of things.

Seek Wise Decisions

We do not need Byzantine (ancient and/or obsolete) artificial laws. Seek out wise decisions instead.

Heighten the Awareness, then Implement Plan

First, heighten the awareness of the coming evolutionary umbrella framework. Then replace the historical construct based on the Nexus Pentarchy Prime Transitional Implementation Plan.

The Power Rests with Us

Do not be discouraged with others' beliefs having views whereby those in privileged circles have the real power. The truth is that with pentarchy primes, the power rests with the vast majority of members in the societal pool. The power rests with us.

Learn Different Ways to Encompass

For a freer and higher just and greater society, remove land and territory jurisdictions. It will be found to be more encompassing towards sentient awareness. Learn different ways to encompass all sentients.

Obsolete Border Containment

Our sentient pursuits to be set free and to mold a much greater and evolved society based on wisdom will make border containment governments obsolete.

Still Standing

Some may be asking me to remain the way I am by insisting that I remain standing still. I prefer to evolve to greater and greater understanding and not be stuck in time. I am still standing.

Do Not Go Back

When there are major Earth changes, choose not to go back to a primitive historical societal existence. Choose a sentient existence.

Pentarchy Prime Challenges

Alternatives, Choices, and Diversities

We need alternatives, choices, and diversities. Incorporating these into our framework will provide us with optimum and unobstructed journeys. We assist each other at different times during our journeys. This is very exciting!

Prime Directives Prior to Universal Foundation

Prime directives will not include investigative findings activities before there is universal prime foundations so that the archival library can continue to operate in a benign non-interference way with non-prime foundations.

The Value of Trust

When a lie is used as an excuse for one's safety net reasons, it is no excuse. Trust is valued more. Consider not commenting at all.

The Healing Approach

Integration into umbrella primes is the healing approach to those entities with imbalance societal pool integration behaviors is promoted and not the condemnation of labeled entities for life.

Business Entity

In primes, no corporation will exist as a unique "business entity". Only a consortium of prime members is recognized. Prime members perform duty caretaker roles in concert for a greater goal and outcome.

Bail Opted Out

The concept of "bail" for a member's release prior to a trial for grave judicial charges has no meaning in pentarchy prime framework. When non-grave harmful acts determined to be in violation, no bail option is needed for release within twenty-five hours. For grave harmful acts, release is when a prime directive opinion and remedies are crafted for one or more participants when a high level of certainty is not made, and not before.

Minimal Inteference

The premise of pentarchy prime is not the construction and maintenance of artificial constructs. The premise is to select the wisest of caretakers in positions defined as being essential for prime health. Micromanaging these prime caretakers by leader caretakers will prove to be counter-productive. It is normally wise to stay out of their way. Restrict interference during those occasions when a caretaker is in violation of prime directives or tenets.

Nature's Dis-eases

To be caretakers of nature is to be promoters of finding cures for dis-eases found in our nature's cornucopia.

Environmental Usage

Geographical (natural) environmental usage will be under the auspices of the umbrella prime based on the Rule-of-Five.

Withholding Information

Prime directives are created based on available information. Those caretakers who withhold information that inhibits the crafting of wiser prime directives will normally be removed from their duty caretaking positions.

In the Most Expeditious Manner

Prime directives are to be completed in the most expeditious manner.

Diverse Transportation Modes

Efficient architectural access routes infrastructure is essential for a vibrant nexus. Ensure diverse modes of transportation. Expand infrastructures that promote high occupancies using fewer transport vehicles. Close to one hundred percent of sentients in the Nexus Prime ought to have access to at least one type of transport system.

Quarantined Primes

For a specified period of time, a prime can be quarantine in response to a grave contagion. The proximity pool (prime) can choose to opt out of health treatments given by ascension degree prime if the proximity pool agrees with being in a state of quarantine until a level of certainty that the proximity pool is cleared of the contagion. In general, a member can be permitted in. However, a member is permitted out when compliance to health treatments are made. The premise for the rights of groups applies in these instances.

Quarantine Option

Quarantine members of a degree prime umbrella when an ascension prime directive requires a health related preventive medicine or inoculation to be taken by all umbrella members and the particular degree prime umbrella does not want to participate. Quarantine in this example means not being able to partake in ascension prime associations and movements. In this way an umbrella prime at any degree can be autonomous when very strong objections are raised.

Harmonic Balances

When living creatures are in human (sentient) care for a reasonable amount of time, then continuation of that care is essential for harmonic balances.

Arriving at Destination

A key to success for pentarchy primes is to have various modes of transportation. There must be viability for all modes and not be primarily of one or two modes. Alternatives ought to be pursued so that they can be accessible to all in one form or another. In this way, balance will be achieved in promoting spiritual development for all when transportation access to all is available to assist in arriving at the final destination being sought.

Not a Constant

Being humane and kind to a living creature even when the time is brief because of forces beyond one's control will go a long way for the creature's corporeal sojourns in other times. The recall that cruelty was or is not a constant nor a universal norm provides a ray of hope and ultimately peace for all involved. Choose hope and give it a try. You are indeed advancing to spiritual graduation.

No More Relevance

There are those who think that the notion regarding the survival of Homo sapiens is paramount to survival of other species. Using this premise, extinguishing of other species is of little consequence, or so it goes. Once this occurred, the belief is that all species that came before and have been extinguished have no more relevance. With this notion, the truth is that neither do we.

Otherwise, Life will Collapse

The diversity of other species made it possible for Homo sapiens to appear and thrive. For Homo sapiens to continue, provide opportunities and environments for these other species to continue. Otherwise, life will collapse for all. How will you choose?

Access to Natural Habitats

When it comes to natural habitats, wide uses of fence construction are prohibited so that no artificial barrier can block nature's creatures in crossing into their natural habitats. Our propagation depends on theirs. There may be rare exceptions like possibly the one historical example in Australia of the Twentieth Century whereby non-native inhabitants, such as the rabbits, were introduced by sentients that had a profound impact of the surroundings. In this case, a great fence cutting across the entire length of a territorial was constructed so that territories that are not already affected are kept that way.

To Gently Escape

In general, nature creatures "humanely" kill their prey before the feast so as to allow the spirit to gently escape. Keep this in mind when the livestock is killed for food.

Urgency and Available Information

It is recognized that prime directives are based on what is available information. However, since the premise of primes is that decisions will not condemn, there is no hesitation in arriving at prime directives when an urgency is present. It is a given that prime directives can be adjusted when more convincing and more available information is discovered requiring a revised prime directive or revocation. In short, when there is an urgency that exists, move from a holding position. To be in such a position may cause more harmful results than moving in a direction that yields more tranquil results.

On Nature's Terms

Entities classified as adults do have choices to meld with nature. This privilege is to be done on nature's terms. Only minimal firepower weapons can be used as part of the survival gear. The choice to be with nature is theirs along. When entities are not developed sufficiently for adult classification, pre-adult caretakers will accompanied them using more than minimal firepower weapons to protect them only. No hunting will be done using these weapons.

Ample Developmental Adjustment

When duty caretakers are selected to oversee the caretaking of nature's creatures, ample developmental adjustment will occur for those in captivity before they are released from captivity and back into to wild.

Take Only What is Needed

It has often been suggested that we treat all of nature humanely. Others will suggest that nature shows cruelty when the hunter pursues its prey and that we "humans" are just performing the hunting and gathering activities that is similarly observed in nature. This is a convincing argument. However, nature's species take only what they need. At times, the take is small or none at all. Also, if we "humans" are truly sentients, then awareness of understanding leads us to be caretakers and to be aware of humane ways of interacting with nature. In this way, this will minimize the transitional pain to non-corporeal existence when we are sufficiently satisfying our sustenance needs. Not having this view as our goal will transform earth into a barren environment over time.

The Lost is Felt

Consider the affect that the following will have before you decide on it. Tapping water from the Great Lakes and diverting the water to distant reservoir will have an effect. Nature will make an adjustment to put water elsewhere from the man-made reservoir. The lost will be felt at both locations.

Umbrella Prime Credits

Umbrella prime credits earned, instead of currencies, can be used and transferred only by the members within the umbrella prime.

Road System "Jurisdiction"

It is obvious with historical land boundary overlapping systems to identify land umbrella "jurisdiction", for example, road systems. They are easily identified with route markers to represent locale, regional, or other spanning boundary domains. However, the construction and maintenance of these systems have overlapping involvement. This illustrates the multiplicity and the confusion that occurs with this construct. Instead, the road system with a particular designator will be under the auspices of the umbrella spanning the system and no other. In this way, there is no avoiding responsibility. This is important for all travel routes because travelers will not be subjected to conflicting governance rules and guidelines. Users of a particular umbrella prime route system and who have blatant violations of its use will result in removal of travel route privileges for all routes within the umbrella prime governance.

The Span of Transportation Routes

In historical times, a country can block entry of transportation vehicles for whatever reason. This island mentality does not exist in pentarchy prime framework. An umbrella prime that spans the transportation routes has the prime directive creation empowerment and all subsequent responsibilities for their viability. When transportation routes span greater than the original umbrella prime, the next ascension degree prime or a greater degree prime that spans them has the prime directive creation empowerment and all subsequent responsibilities for their viability.

Exile-in-confinement Duration

Those who have the propensity for harmful activities will be kept from the general member population. The duration is long. Extinguishing of corporeal life will result in a very long exile-in-confinement duration.

Degrees of Isolation

Historical references called "prison inmates" who exhibit continual violent activities may be placed in greater degrees of pool isolation. There are to be no mixing of inmates with different degree designations.

Initiating a Request for Opinion Fitness Test

The member who is initiating a request for a pentarchy prime opinion will only be considered when the member has complied or is complying with all prime directives regarding the member. Exceptions are when grave acts or urgent natural causes are the basis for the request.

A Pressing Concern

It is essential that a member who has been identified with committing grave harmful acts be placed in confinement even when there is not a high level of certainty that she indeed is the one. The exception is when she is defending herself from another who is committing grave harmful acts. Not allowing members from being confined who have the propensity for committing grave harmful acts be allowed to slip through is a pressing concern to the health and welfare of all in the nexus prime. When a member of the nexus prime is held in confinement for suspected violent harmful acts performed by this member, the member must be released at five years or less when superior facts and evidence are not available or discovered.

By placing a member in confinement when reasonable facts and evidences are available and yet release the member after a relatively short period of time will dramatically reduce the chances that a member is released on a technicality as was practiced in historical legal frameworks. Also, the notion that a member can avoid being caught is dramatically reduced because the vast majority of members will be less likely to test the boundary of the notion of not getting "caught".

Designation Permanence

Children who are abandoned or are runaways will have child duty caretakers immediately assigned to them when discovered. Current child caretakers are temporarily removed from designations until there is a high certainty for effective child caretaking duties to exist or sound prime directives and remedies are made, which significantly changes the permanence of the current child caretaker's designations. Those who are adept in seeing through children's eyes will evaluate and recommend remedies.

Sustain a Cornucopia

Waste not and Earth can produce and sustain a cornucopia of wonderful and marvelous life sustaining goods.

A Test Trial Run

Time will show that the most mechanized form of a nation-state will be unworkable when Earth changes occur. Land lords will find their property values evaporate. The Foundation Book of Primes can be used as a guidebook for pools of entities to have peace and tranquillity. Why wait for these events to occur? Take it for a test trial run today.

Under Normal Conditions

The need to demonstrate fitness regarding compliance to prime directives is high. Removal of entities who are in non-compliance will be done using, under normal conditions, any and all non-violent means necessary. The exception is when grave harmful acts are occurring or there is a high degree of certainty that they will occur. In these situations, sufficient forceful remedies are necessary by Nexus Rapid Response Teams.

Remedies in Multitudes

There is very little concern regarding the guarded "secrets" of historical "secret agencies". The prime importance for us is for prime directives to be fully understood and implemented throughout umbrella prime. These prime directives can be crafted based on available information and not the complete informational collection when they are based on basic prime tenets. The unwise secret agencies actions will be exposed in time with corrective prime directives crafted. Those who failed or neglected earlier prime directives will have remedial plans crafted with more stern corrective and penalty remedies in multitudes of the earlier directives. Wise leader caretakers are not to be mocked with defiance by prime directive recipients. This includes resolutions when one or more recipients have transferred into non-corporeal form. Those who benefited from such violations will have their portions returned to recipients' domain for resolution.

Many Millennia War

There will be no promotion of military equipment and personnel in a pentarchy prime framework. Historical promotion of military equipment and personnel always lead to war. The outcome was always the same. Upon reflection of history, it was a single war that spanned many millennia with temporary truces along the way. The nexus prime will maintain instruments of Nexus Rapid Response Teams to reduce all grave harmful directing events by members to zero using sufficient force to make this so. Greater use of force is not to be considered when reduced levels of force have not been given consideration and attempted for result evaluation.

Identification is Key

Condemn not. However, identification of privilege abusers is a valid concern. Let the matter be clearly stated. Abusers will have their privileges revoked for a significant period of time.

Zoned for Natural Habitat

Land zoned for natural habitat. This means that no large or long artificial barriers are to be installed for significant sized land, water, air, and space surroundings when few sentients resides. When artificial barriers are constructed for safety and security reasons, the perimeters will tightly surround sentient activities. Be mindful that we are caretakers for a larger whole.

Less Than Harmful Violation

When the offender of a less than harmful violation chooses not to be present for violation review evaluation, testimony by those present can commence and be completed for issue resolution outcome. When rendered, the terms of the remedies are implemented. Compliance of these terms must be fulfilled. As is shown, outcomes are based on available information. Abstention by the offender indicates a choice that she has made. Only when the abstentions are due to extreme hardships can the outcomes be revised with additional information provided by those who have abstained.

Solidify Completeness

Prime directives covering members will be complied with in time even when the explicit recall of them has not surfaced to the covered members' consciousness. The collective consciousness will in time solidify completeness.

No Ban on Risks

There will be no ban on risks made by members of a group when no other group is affected. The exception is those who are being cared for due to reasons of being not of sufficient maturity for self-directing activities under their own volition.

Lessen and Cheapen

The extinguishing of corporeal life shall be the greatest of all harmful acts in a pentarchy prime. No other act will be equal to or greater than this gravest of act. For to make other acts at the same gravity will lessen and cheapen the extinguishing of corporeal life.

Usage of Resources

Usage of resources is based on fitness and certification in their use. Fitness means wherewithal, the right mix of duty caretaker characteristics, wise resource selection, and sufficient collection tests. Certification means the minimum rating of the fitness tests. Levels of certifications may be considered for rating grade distinctions.

Power Spread

If one is focus on what power exist today, then one cannot see the baton being passed tomorrow. What would one like to see? Should the power be concentrated or spread throughout the umbrella.

Development Centers

Provide development centers for all those who desire further development. Each center will be guided by its own defined framework based on developmental needs.

Oversees All

Ensure that wise leader caretakers oversee all.

Sentient Renaissance

I Cannot Make You Hear

I can utter the words. However, I cannot make you hear them! Do you hear them now?

The Recipient

There may be an issue or two that I am diametrically opposite to from your point of view. However, your limited view of the issues will set into motion a recipient of your decisions and actions. I value the passion that you sincerely expend in arriving at wise resolutions and your resolve in maintaining them. What you don't know is this. You are the recipient!

Released from Garb

With livestock, the meat does not react after the livestock has been butchered. Its spirit has been released. As sentients occupying a corporeal garb, we do the same.

Corporeal Experience

Corporeal experience offers the opportunity to develop one's self in the pursuit for understanding and insights even when they are hidden from view. They are only hidden when total immersion in corporeal garb is chosen. To reach beyond this does require faith in a realm beyond one's own, which is not that easy in the beginning of one's journey. It requires one to be aware of the signposts and markings along the way. Once understanding and insights are known, one will have certainty and be surprised why other sojourners cannot notice these same signposts and markings.

Merit Evaluation

Every member past, present, and future will be evaluated by her merits when there are questions regarding actions that resulted in harm to others.

Their Essence

The words that are spoken (or written) here will resonate to those sentients who are atone to their essence.

Intoxicating

The state of being a sentient is very intoxicating.

Spiritual Observations

The Door is Open

The more one pursues insights and "what-is" notions, the more the door of insights and understanding is opened to her. In time, all of your questions will be answered. Your level of passion and sincerity determine the duration.

In the Here and Now

Wouldn't you like to create the environment that will provide the greatest peace and joy? You can if the will be there in the here and now.

The Will to Aspire

Those who wish to aspire, will.

Spiritual Health

The elitists material wealth that is hoarded will not help much in their spiritual health.

In Sharper Focus

Activities focused on distractions for material wealth will then yield to spiritual development that will go out of focus. Activities focused on enlightenment will then yield to spiritual development that will come into sharper focus. Is it clear to you now?

Become a Healer

There is no healing when there is condemnation. Now, are you a healer?

Earth Suit

Enjoy your Earth suit.

Origins of Life Instructions

Looking all around on spaceship Earth, one will notice thousands of species on land, in the air, and in the water. All take their sustenance from the land, air, and sea. The difference being that each has a set of life instructions for living. The originator of these instructions is ATI.

Harmonizing with Nature

We need to harmonize with nature. This cannot be done by owning and (or) controlling it. Nature is always in control.

Suppression of Corporeal Instincts

Our free will can suppress corporeal instincts that can extinguish the corporeal suit, that is, not fighting back or running when certain life or earth situations occur. There are times when instincts serve us well.

Heard in a Fortress

To have a greater success in passing the word to the most ardent society, I was born in its proximity so that the word can be heard by the most fortress nation in the world.

Island Stasis

Your island stasis is being disturbed. To survive and thrive, you must wake up.

Spiritual Breath

Their historical beliefs are choking all of their spiritual breath. Choose to take deep breaths.

Staying in the Ring

Your arena will keep you in the ring until all players cease their arrogant ways of eliminating their opponents. There will always be opponents when fighting is part of your belief system.

Glorious Events Received

To some, war is glorious. The element not understood by them is that they will experience in kind that which they thought were glorious events. Each of us then chooses the events that we will participate in.

When One Condemns

In time, those who condemn are also condemned. In time, many will be confused when they find themselves in situations of being condemned. Universal law states; condemn not or you shall be condemned.

Atonement and Salvation

Grace comes to being after great atonement. Serving your fellow entities is the way to salvation.

All You See

If that is all you see, then that is all you can discover.

Metamorphosing

I am metamorphosing into something greater!

Separate and Yet Share

If one chooses to remain in the material realm, graduation to a higher level of understanding will require many sojourns. Have comfort in the truth that everyone who has been assigned to this plane has not been able to do it in just one journey. Keep in mind that the lure to this plane was and still is very enticing, don't you think? At one "time", when we inhabited our human form in earlier forms, we knew about our spiritual realm and in "reality", we were able to have communications with those entities who were waiting in the wings, so to speak. When we lost our "consciousness" was when we chose to be gratified in the experience of this three-dimensional realm and forsake our spiritual at-one-ment with All-That-Is. To be of one mind and body validated our uniqueness and separateness from other entities. At the same time, by having separateness existence from other entities, we can also share experiences with others and not be alone. One will note that insanity by some resulted from their belief system that they are cursed in their human form because they were condemned into this realm not of their own choosing. If one is perceptive, one will notice that there are always caretakers who will assist those in need. These caretakers freely volunteer in their vocations. These caretakers recalled their own needs and other caretakers who helped them. The disturbed ones need to recognize that this Earth is here for our spiritual selves in order for each to grow and advanced to the next level of awareness. It is not an easy effort to freely accept on our own free will, the true nature of our own existence with All-That-Is. The lessons for most of us is the notion of giving of ourselves so that others can be guided and helped towards their own higher selves. This must be done on our own free will. It matters not that this notion must be accepted in the shortest possible "time." The truth is that there is no short cut or substitute way. All will attain. One, however, has "all the time in the world." This world will reunite with ATI when all entities enrolled in this world have all harmonized with everything in this world.

A Time of Great Mental Capacities

There is a prevailing view that humans advanced over time. However, if (wo)man existed for thousands of years and has gone through very little genetic change, then great mental capacities have existed during this entire time! What unlocks these capabilities? Self!

Equipped with a Barren Landscape

An Earth, even a barren one, will exist if that is what one needs to develop. A barren landscape awaits for those who need it most.

Free Will is Primary

Entities in corporal form have asked very strongly to ATI as to why ATI did not send anyone to help them find their way back. The reply is that countless spiritual guides did in fact pass through into our realm and lived among us. However, the very same entities that wanted guidance rejected them. The fundamental principle of free will is primary to having guides forced entities to see the light. Hence, your free will ultimately guide you. Where will you go? Is it along the path of darkness or one of light?

Seeing both Sides

Imagine being the most successful business executive who has profit from the labors of others in one sojourn. Imagine being the laborer whose labor is promoting another successful business executive who is profiting off the labors of you and others in another sojourn. One can now "see" both sides. Will this lead to growth in spiritual development or that of being stuck in time on Earth? What do you choose?

Playing by the Rules

Play by the rules, which are the rules of being penalized. That is life! We have heard this before. However, the more important question is this: Whose rules will you subscribe to? Will the rules be artificial (man-made) or natural (ATI)? What set of rules will govern in the final outcome?

Playback

It is very tempting to turn away spiritual development and immersed oneself in corporeal existence. The two frameworks exist simultaneous. However, without the spiritual development, the corporeal existence will replay itself and hence, be stuck in time.

Hidden from View

Without knowing the cause, a centric entity will struggle to a high degree and not comprehend a universal truth or concept. ATI desires not to introduce universal truths or concepts until the spiritual entity is ready. You see, it is being hidden because of her centric view.

The Black Plague

The black plague of Medieval Europe could have wiped out all of mankind, but it didn't. Maybe it was due to folks who did not follow expert advice when their instincts told them differently. Seeking the truths and the way is one's true spiritual path.

Bent on Condemning

Do not be bent on the notion of condemning any entity. The end result of these activities will be the complete destruction for all actors who participate.

Institutions that Crumble

Be careful not to put your beliefs in institutions that can crumble when Earth makes a correction. Put your beliefs in the spirit of all. The spirit endures all Earth changes.

Seeding the Word

Currently for many entities, the ability to paint a better scene for all is ever present. However, the results may require more "time" than an entity has in one sojourn. Awareness of this concept is needed in order for activities to be initiated in the present. With this awareness and active pursuit of beautification and serenity, graduation is assured. Given this, it is wise to set into motion from a standing position the seeding of the Word that will germinate and grow into form and substance for others to be drawn to and reach for. It truly will be an awe and inspiring sight. Choose to aspire!

Exist for All Times

There is a belief that individuals are born, live their lives, and then die over their lifetimes while governments live on. The truth is that governments are short lived and spiritual entities exist for all time.

Cannot be Measured

There is a belief that when "man", for example a group of scientists, produces cell-generating organisms and that these organisms are non-persons. The truth is that there exist "awareness" regarding its surroundings and beyond. Since "man" (a group of scientists) can't measure this, then it is concluded that it doesn't exist. The thinking is that the organism is only a "spontaneous organism". "From Earth comes dirt", is the conclusion. With this premise, "man" (a group of scientists) does not exist either.

Come to Fruition

Having different societies and cultures to exist simultaneous on the third rock from the Sun provides the favorable conditions so that awareness can come to fruition. Free will can choose the outcome. Free will can choose to move towards a higher level of awareness. How do you choose?

Hope in the Recall of Experiences

It is far better for humanity (sentient collective) to treat all of nature with humane (sentient acumen) treatment even when some will be harvested for food. By providing favorable and sustainable conditions and environments, recall of these humane experiences will provide the hope for nature's participants, which will provide the aspiration to a higher level of awareness. Since the happenings did occur, there is precedence that these favorable conditions can occur again. Hence, hope is cultivated, which leads further to your spiritual development as well.

View from a Sandbox

Those who immersed themselves in corporeal realm will have limited vision than those who envelop non-corporeal realm. In the latter, they will have unlimited vision. The former can only play in their own sandboxes of their choosing.

Resembles (Wo)man

There is a notion, that what is created by (wo)man to resemble (wo)man, is not in fact sentient. This is a fallacy. Consider the notion that what is created by ATI to resemble ATI is not in fact ATI. This analogy is also a fallacy. Be not afraid. Awareness of existence keeps one sane when a desire to continually graduate to higher and higher levels of awareness is lit. A spiritual flame will set you free.

A Constant Flame

A destructive corporeal experience requires a balance with a constructive corporeal experience. Time and patience are required for the latter. Consider that a flame burns what appears to be for a very long time. The flame builds very quickly before becoming constant.

Celebration of the Spirit

It may seem a tragedy for an entity to go through a long and abusive sojourn. The entity may even constantly experience new abuses at every corner. And yet at the same time, the entity does what she knows is right. This example is a celebration of the spirit that can go beyond material realm and reach escape velocity.

Portals into Earth's Sphere of Influence

Portals into Earth's sphere of influence exist. Often spiritual entities wish to join you on your journey. That is, to be a part of your experiences. Consider allowing them to walk along side you.

Originator of Ideas

There will be those that proclaim that they are the originator of ideas and not you. In the collective consciousness of all, we were all contributors to their promotion. Therefore, it is extremely important to speak the words so that you are certain that the words are spoken at least once.

Awakening to an Awareness

One will notice that those who want to escape from corporeal form do not want to be told of a spiritual evolvement. In fact, they will resent being lead to their awakening of this awareness.

Time Given to You

There are those who will say that the twilight years mean the slowing down of learning and other activities. On the contrary, those who have new or renewed pursuits will prepare themselves for what lies ahead, be it spiritual or another sojourn. There are times when working out a problem or situation is being done in one sojourn and then the favorable results are used in another (simultaneous) sojourn. In summary, take advantage of the "time" given to you.

Not Anchored to No Avail

If one tunes a radio to locate a signal, there is a variety from noisy and faint background to strong signal strength ones. When one tunes into a stronger signal, the noise is minimal and the message is clear. This is analogous to when an entity goes in and out of corporeal realm. For some, this corporeal realm is tuned out to reach a higher realm. For those immersed in the corporeal realm, these not fully anchored entities are given many identifications, such as, voodoo, witches, insane, soothsayer, mentally ill, etc. These non-anchored entities did not want to enter corporeal realm to no avail. Be patient when dealing with them. The environments that will provide the conditions to help "heal" these entities' non-participation states are those of non-condemning ones that promote growth in spiritual development.

Insights that are Elusive

There are those who are awed regarding insights that are elusive to them. Those with higher level of insights need not imitate those who are not, just for the sake of assimilating. Be grateful that you have these insights and spend little effort in convincing those who do not. Be mindful and respectful that each is at her particular level of awareness.

Dwarfed by One's Action

There is a notion that just because an action is legal, one has every right to execute it with impunity. One may appear to have legal support for such an action. However, the action may dwarf one's spiritual development with ATI. Why would anyone want to do that?

Minimize Spiritual Hurt

Those who give and carry out orders to execute anyone in captivity are actually cowards. Their "power" is hollow. The opportunity is actually this. It is to find ways to minimize spiritual hurt for all concerned. This will greatly help all those who are stuck in time.

Wonderful and Spectacular

One will say, "I believe" and still be surprised that one's belief do come into fruition and is materialized. Choose a belief that will come to fruition and materialize that which is most wonderful and in most spectacular surroundings.

Opportunity for Spiritual Awareness

It is not that those who remain are the chosen ones. Rather, it is that you are given the opportunities to continue your developmental spiritual awareness pursuits. Best wishes on your journeys.

To Reach Escape Velocity

Everyone will need to release her belief in artificial (man-made) constructs and believe in higher levels of awareness in order to reach escape velocity. The latter will help return one to a realm of an even greater awareness.

So the Saying Goes

"God works in mysterious ways", so the saying goes. This is not accurate. We work in mysterious ways. The saying is due to our lack of insights. As soon as we are ready and are able to receive insights, the ways are mysterious no more! When only a few gain insights, the others will continue to believe that "God works in mysterious ways", which will continue to be posed to sentients again and again until a desire to reach for a greater understanding is made.

Electrifying Events

As higher and higher levels of awareness are attained, one will understand that the word is ever present for anyone to receive the word. All it takes is for one to be receptive. This may require a high degree of spiritual development. The path is not always easy for those who see the world as based centrally around them. In this centric-based framework, one is not mobile. Rather, one is anchored to ground. On the other hand, numerous electrifying events take place in a spiritual development framework.

Return Visits

There are those who think that the specie known as Homo sapiens are the owners of this planet to do with it whatever this specie wants. In truth, we are visitors for a short stay. If we neglect this planet, then on our subsequent return visits, the planet will be a very different place to stay than the one that we remember when we have recall of them. This will jolt us. The changes encountered arise out of the activities and actions of your earlier visits.

Entity's Truest Power

The set of exercises and activities in making choices by an entity is the truest power in corporeal existence.

Encourage Entities On

More favorable conditions on Earth will be forthcoming. However, when none or little entity growth occurs, a correction of Earth conditions will occur to encourage entities to continue with spiritual growth. Watch for them.

Advances Hidden From View

Insights will be hidden from view until sufficient growth exists to permit further advances in spiritual development.

Sponsors and Guides

Entities in spiritual realm do not find Earth corporeal realm that much interesting than the realm that they are in. However, they have agreed to sponsor and be guides when the interest is there by Earth corporeal entities. Do take advantage of them!

An Earth Correction

It doesn't matter what exists today. Earth will go through a correction to clear up matters in order to bring forth a new dawn.

Finish Line

One goes on a journey through life from beginning to end. To reach the end is quite an accomplishment. One might say, I made it! It is a celebration! However, don't cut it short. If you do, there is no celebration or it is greatly diminished! The finish line will surprise you when you go all the way.

Onto the Least

Who so ever do it onto the least of thee, do it onto me.

It is Perfectly Okay!

It is perfectly okay to be sentient. It is perfectly okay to have awareness. It is perfectly okay to return from whence we came. There is no longer fear once these insights are known. It is perfectly okay!

View from Beyond

Once departed from this Earth, other realities come into focus.

The Greatest

The spirit is greater than any corporeal existence. The greatest is within you.

You are not Alone

It is important to you that you utter the word. If you do not, how can anyone else know of its existence? By uttering the word, you will have set into motion a profound broadcast that will reach way beyond your horizontal reach. Your word projection may be beyond your understanding. However, it will be felt far and wide. I will feel it. I will know of its existence. You are not alone. Thank you for being courageous.

All-That-Is (ATI) - Initial Collection

Pronunciation of ATI:

‾ ´‾

a - ti

Two syllables. First syllable, long "a". Second syllable, short "ta" followed by long "I". Strong accent is on the second syllable.

ATI Ceremonial Gesture

1. Body is standing erect with feet flat on the ground and comfortably separated.
2. Hands come together. They clap flat in front of chest with fingers together, straight, and pointing upward. Arms from hand to elbows are parallel to the ground or perpendicular to torso.
3. Hands are raised over the head following the spine.
4. Separate the hands and arc up and out making a circle back together. The final position is the start of step two above with hands together.

ATI Ceremonial Hand Symbol

The fingers of the hand are curled and together into the palm of the hand in the middle. The tips of the fingers follow the fleshy part of the base of the thumb with the thumb pointing straight up (ascending). The hand is straight and not bent at the wrist facing forward to others. The arm is bent at the elbow in small social gatherings. The arm is not bent and raised in large social gatherings. The final shape of the hand resembles a triangle with the pointing thumb being one point of the triangle and the other two points, which are the rounded corners of the hand triangle, are at the base.

The symbol represents solidarity and support for each other. The foundation support for the thumb (symbolic of the other leader caretakers) assists the thumb (symbolic of the ascension leader caretaker selected) in the ascension.

ATI is Not Mocked

ATI is not mocked, and neither am I.

The Limit

One might say that All-That-Is is the limit!

Thoughts Repository

Afraid of Your Beliefs

Do not be afraid. It is only your beliefs. Maybe there are notions to work out, which is why you may be afraid. Maybe the things that you hold so dear are the very ones that ground you and cause you to be afraid. Let go of them.

Choose to Believe

You believe what you want to believe. Hence, you believe what you choose.

What You Believe

What do you believe in? Be careful what you believe in. Your beliefs create your world!

Foolish Warriors

There are no great warriors, just foolish ones.

Virtual

Do you believe that virtual laws will protect us? Why not instead permit sentients to be our protectors? There is nothing virtual about this framework.

A Better Fit

Consider not thinking yourself as a member of the masses. Start thinking yourself as a member of an umbrella prime. The right size umbrella prime can better fit your needs.

An Objective for Society

Just like a large insurance pool of policy holders provides a greater chance of surviving major emergencies, a greater societal pool of members provides a greater chance of surviving and living in peace. Isn't peace the true objective for society?

Lighten the Weight

Do consider this. Responsibilities for wise decisions can rest on all of us and not just the few who have in historical references hoarded power away from us. In this way, any problem can be more easily handled when more members are involved to lighten the weight of the problem.

Which would You Choose

Are we or are we not a sentient friendly society? Which would you choose?

To be Anchored to Rock

It is important to evolve to a higher level of understanding. To hold tightly to a land lord system will keep one anchored to rock. Would not one desire to travel the universe instead? There are wonders that await you!

Memberships

I do not tell members what to do. They are free to choose their own memberships.

Fear Replaced with Peace

Today, entities have fear. It will be replaced with peace once entities know the insightful reasons for their Earth experiences.

Take Care of Earth

If we don't take care of Earth, Earth will not take care of us. Take care of Earth.

A Chance to Make it Happen

The utterance of the word starts into motion the changes it speaks of. When you utter the word, the resultant effect can have a greater chance of happening.

Moved With a Thought

You may say that the simple act of making a decision holds no action until the decision is carried out. Consider this. Doesn't making a decision require thought and energy on your part? If so, then the action has taken place. The physical is the result when time is added into the mix. To have immediacy or immediate reaction is not the best way. The world is moved with a thought. You may not even be aware that this is being done!

A Collection of Thoughts

A collection of thoughts will yield to a change in weather. A collection of decisions will yield to Earth changes. A collection of the same decision made by many creates a New World. This is the way towards All-That-Is and you are a part of it! The choice is yours. The choice is clear.

The Word that Silences

The word silences any weapon, even weapons of massive destruction.

Provide Room for Passage

When there is condemnation by one to another, the other will think that the passage is obstructed and there is no other option. Provide room for one's passage.

When the Time is Right

There have been many "great comfortable societies" that came and went when comfort was the primary goal of entities and not the use of favorable environments to ponder and explore spiritual awareness. A return to more uncomfortable surroundings was then reestablished for them. Those who did grow returned to favorable conditions. This illustrates what is meant by, "When the time is right."

Survival Instincts

Survival instincts means hunted like an animal.

Your Chosen Path

Long suffering illnesses may be avenues for atonement for some entities due to the opportunity to be in close proximity to inspirational awareness environments so as to entice an entity to a realm that most closely resemble ATI realm. Hence, if this is to be your path that you have chosen, then it will present itself. What path do you choose?

Family Type

Do you believe in a nature-derived family or an artificially-derived surrogate one?

Putting in More Distance

A system that condemns will be extinguished. It endures when we continue to feed its fire. Taking this condemning course will put more distance between you and ATI.

A Business that Backfires

We must get out of the condemning business. It results in spiritual backfires.

There is No Peace with Hate

An entity's hate is keeping same from having peace. Hence, there is no peace with hate.

Duration to get in or out

However long it took you to get into a situation, for whatever reasons that might be, may take you just as long to get out of it.

Void of Feelings

Do you think we should be void of feelings with our "representative government" that reinforces the elitist premise that promote terrorism everywhere? Having no feelings will keep you in chains in ways that are not apparent in the present. The outcome of your deeds awaits you.

Vantage Point Perspective

You are here to get answers from me. What types of answers are you really looking for? If I speak words that you do not understand, than you either need more preparations for understanding or the answers from me are not acceptable in your belief framework. Maybe you should stay in yours until you choose to seek out a different vantage point perspective.

The Ebb and Flow of Civilizations

History shows that civilizations come and go. And why is this? Consider this: At the height of a civilization is when many entities have reached graduation to the next level. When there is calamity is when recent arrivals chose to be set back a grade and continue to take in the carnal yearnings of being rulers over others.

For Spiritual Health Reasons

We have allowances for mental health reasons. To advance to a higher level of awareness, the "legal" allowances for spiritual health reasons will elevate all of society.

Observe Children Grow

By observing children, one can also let go of the confines promoted by self that holds one from growth.

The Extinction of (Wo)man

Nature will determine the extinction of species, not "(wo)mankind". When (wo)man interferes, then (wo)man becomes extinct!

Analogy for Advancement

Consider this analogy. Computers at one time use extensively vacuum tubes, which used a lot of electricity. Engineers wanted to continue with its applications even though transistors proved far cheaper to produce and operate. Letting go of something that is familiar for something that can advance society is always difficult. However, it must be done for further developmental advances to be realized. Hence, even our current familiar form of feudal states must be shut down and have installed a far better system to take its place in order for our earth sphere of influence to be one of peace and tranquillity.

Stuck in the Past

Members of the judiciary and their soldiers dwell on the past in placing blame. It is folly to expect any kind of vision to originate from them. Choose wise leader caretakers to accelerate your understanding towards higher and higher levels of awareness.

Access to Basic Corporeal Needs

It is still barbarism at its highest (maximum) form to deny access to basic corporeal needs. Some may consider it acceptable to snuff out another entity. It is wiser not to take their lead. Their own famine awaits them.

Early Recalls

Some entities preferred that the books I author be "pure" in the topic that is covered. Indeed! This book by this author also focuses on the spiritual. The "basic" summary book is an experience in the many threads of thoughts that can be contemplated at the same time. Taking one thread can occupy an entity for a lifetime. Imagine what many life times can do. With spiritual at-one-ment, recalls of many threads are possible. Take heart! All will have keen recall of them in time. The question is how soon do you want to begin your recall?

Discovery Lead to an Awakened State

Do not condemn yourself upon the discovery that you may have caused atrocities toward others. Look around you and you will observe that others fell in the same abyss as you have done. You need to ask yourself. How many times will I repeat the same before waking up to a higher level of awareness and ultimately, graduation? Take heart. Your discovery did lead you to your own awakened state.

Total Eradication

History will not look upon terrorism very kindly in all its many forms. There is no escaping the end result, which is total eradication.

Artificial World

The notion that land lords own their subjects is pure fiction and artificial. The fiction comes to life in your environment of beliefs. You create your own artificial world.

Not Yet Sentient

Doctors who execute babies during partial birth abortions are no different then the doctors who perform horrific experiments on groups of state-defined undesirables and other condemned persons during the historical era referred to as Nazis Germany. Both were sanctioned by the state. It is easy for the state to condemn members of the societal pool because they are defined as non-sentient. Why would sentients permit this to happen? Could it be that members are shaped into this false (artificial) belief system by the state? Or could it be that members are not sentients after all!

No Escaping from the Truth

There may be those who say that atrocities in the past are not our concern because they are in the "past". The truth is that the atrocities completed in the past result in the brewing of the truths to be known in the present. Then these truths are to be acknowledged and the history recordings be reviewed and corrected to reflect the identification of those who promoted and carried out the atrocities. In this way, these harmful acting entities did not escape their fate by their corporeal expiration. The fallacy that no one will notice or find the clues is just that. By suppressing truths, you become the participants to the atrocities. Even "great leaders" that are long gone will get their historical recordings accurately reflected. By refusing to examine actual historical events, we perpetuate violent belief systems. These systems must expire and be replaced with systems far greater and inclusive of all sentient entities. Be mindful that no entity can be snuffed out.

Sad Commentary

We will not glorify genocide of any kind even the historical referenced ones. It is a sad commentary to glorify the parties who have. No army that committed atrocities will be given glorious historical status.

Is Life Real

We have motion pictures and sound. We say that this is not real and only a movie. However, is life real or a motion picture with sound?

Chasing Their Own Tails

Those who view themselves as experts who are above the masses in society are actually following a circular path over time and not even realize that they are chasing their own tails.

Not a Commune

It is unclear why one would think that a pentarchy prime is a commune. The affiliation is not based on a single political premise or monolith. The affiliation you choose is your own. My advice to anyone is to choose wisely.

In All Manner of

When harmful acts or there is a high certainty that harmful acts are imminent, then the Nexus Rapid Response Teams are deployed to reduce all harmful acts being committed to zero. We condemn no one. However, we are not to promote harmful acts if at all possible in reducing harmful acts to zero. We are to promote peace and tranquillity in all manners of form and degree.

Taking a Higher or Lower Path

The notion that if others do something that may be legal but not wise, then the feeling is that they can do it too. However, one can choose to take a path of higher and higher levels of awareness and not the path of stagnation or a path towards lower and lower levels of awareness. One will not be aware that the losses of her own awareness and recall are due to taking the latter approach.

Unprotected

When only "citizens" of one nation-state are protected exclusively, then no one is protected. These citizens, who look out will in time, look in and be unprotected.

Dichotomy

In a "civilized" society, it is permissible, as can be found in a sporting event such as boxing, to knock the opponent's head off in the arena. However, outside the arena, it is not! What a strange dichotomy to be in.

Exposed

If I am assassinated, it is highly likely that it is due to my striking a chord of truth. Those who are the conspirators were provoked because of their own houses of cards are falling. They are exposed.

How to Continue a Thriving Cycle

If you think there will always be someone to take your place with violent activities, then your beliefs will keep the thriving cycle going. However, as more sentients leave these activities, the diehards will extinguish each other.

Not as Vibrant over Time

Cell division is not as vibrant over time. The environment likewise is not as vibrant over time when it is divided up again and again. Consider returning it to its pristine beauty.

The Next Correction

There are still those believers who believe that by being anchored to rock (Earth) or land that their properties are secured. This complacency lasts until the next Earth correctional cycle event.

Correlation

There seems to be a correlation between mental decisions and events, even for those that are distance ones.

Sustainable Growth

Coexist and blend in with nature. Promote sustainable growth up to a level before the saturation level.

A Ray of Hope

An observation is made. A mentally challenged corporeal entity will, on occasion, blurt out an insight that is quite revealing! A ray of hope can occur for any entity when the knowledge of ATI can be tapped.

One's Actions and Inactions

One will be judged on one's actions and inactions.

Does it onto Me

Whoever does it onto the least of thee, does it onto me.

The Survival of All in Diversity

Do not wish the death of any specie, which also includes your own. Diversity promotes the survival of all.

You are the Foundation

You are empowered to make your own decisions. "Follow me" leadership has no meaning in a prime framework. You are the foundation for all things that impacts your pursuits from the smallest to the largest. I cannot interfere in your prime directive creations. The exception is when they violate basic prime tenets. In grave harmful situations, Nexus Rapid Response Teams go into action. The response is swift because we require it to be so.

Pick Wise Sentients

Wise decisions are made by wise sentients. Artificial laws do not effectively result in wise decisions in most cases, which make slaves of us for feudal lords. I pick wise sentients.

Tunnel Vision

Some of you are still asking questions pertaining to propping up feudal states viability. This means that you still have tunnel vision. I need to see more.

Not as Nomads

There are sentients who travel the world and beyond. They are not as nomads, by as guests and visitors. Welcome them whenever they pass your way.

A Kind of Freedom

There is a kind of freedom experienced for a member when the judicial system overrate the condemnation of the member of the society pool because of the insistence that the condemned member is to be condemned for life when a felony for a non harmful act sentence is ordered. This major life event then permits no more fear of a feudal system that keeps members in check with the threat of being condemned. The feudal system will then be the recipient of its own condemnation. The birth of this result has already been set into motion because of it. Try it for yourself. The hope that is denied is reflected back to the initiator.

Condemn Not!

You don't actually condemn me. It is reflective. You condemn yourself.

The Life of Primes

A prime has a life of its own. You can be a part of this life.

No One is Alone

When we come together as primes, no one is left alone.

Metamorphose into something greater!

With primes, one will find one's self and will metamorphose into something greater!

It Starts With One

I am one entity. I need four more to make a prime. This is the start to the propagation of primes.

Prime Rules!

Leader caretakers are supreme to all other systems.

The Decision is Yours

The decision is up to you. What will it be?

Envelop Life

I cannot predict (foretell) what future prime directives will be. I can only tell you that they will ebb and flow just like in life and not like historical cemeteries of laws and rulings. Nature teaches us that. Our decisions ought to envelop life as well.

Easy or Not

This is not to say it is easy. Put it another way, it doesn't mean that it will be easy.

Awakening

It is part of the awakening. If one calls out to others and there is no response, then the others must still be asleep. No need to disturb them. When they are ready, they will wake up.

In Chains

It is our participatory beliefs that are keeping all of us in chains. Leave the chains behind.

Words in Motion

The supreme ability to set the word in motion is present in all entities. What word will you utter?

Your Word is Heard

There may be those among you who feel or believe that your word will not be heard by anyone. The truth is that your word is heard. The important thing is this. Will you pass words of good or of evil? Goodwill will aid you in your spiritual development. Evil will keep you stuck in time with ever increasing difficulties and hardships in your continuum. Your notions will construct the environments to try them out over and over. Why allow evil to anchor you to rock?

The Word has Form

There are those who believe that the word holds no form. The word does have form and has been set into motion. The impact occurs in time. It may appear in the future that the impact occurs all of a sudden. Those who are receptive saw it early on as they followed its path to intersection.

Complete Information

When spiritual training is complete for a particular level of awareness, complete information to an urgent issue may not be needed when reliance on prime directives and spiritual insights are followed. In all cases, wise decisions are supreme to precise expert analysis and conclusions.

Refreshing

Once you join a foundation in the pentarchy prime framework, the experience will grow on you in a positive way. It will become very refreshing to be a part of it.

Understanding

It is not as important in the present that one understands 100% of universal truths. However, to pursue understanding of them is!

Speeding up Graduation

Doing the right thing will speed up graduation.

Water Flows

Consider the concept of rain events that occur followed by the clearing of the clouds followed by the trickling of rainwater into small streams then running into larger streams then running into rivers then running into great oceans and lakes. Water flows. So do our thoughts.

Utterances

The word was set into motion. More words (utterances) followed. It is folly to believe that the word has no affect. The word does have an affect. Review the words written by this author and observe your surroundings for validation. Have you noticed the results? All of this is not by chance. Set the word into motion and see what happens next.

To Move an Idea

Our journeys are discovery and learning ones. To initially articulate ideas is most often the greatest push for these ideas. A burst of energy is needed to get an idea to move from a stopped or dormant state. To move an idea along faster requires not as much energy. Once in motion, the idea will continue on its own until the desire and passion ceases.

Incremental Word Affect

The power of the word penetrates and chips away at any obstacle that may exist. The dramatic results do not normally occur in the near future. However, they do occur in time even when you lose interest of or have forgotten it. When the changes occur incrementally, they have more permanence and produce more lasting results. Be proud of your accomplishments. Thank you from all of us for trying.

Sentient Affirmations

Hope for Others

One can say, I did it for me! The hope is that others can benefit as well.

Making All of the Decisions

I won't be making all of the decisions. We will. In this way, we made it so!

A Catalyst for Actors

I am just the catalyst. You are the actors who will make it so.

For Ourselves

Be empowered and let us create wise decisions for ourselves.

A Signpost

I am a signpost. I can point you along the way. The journey is initially yours to take to be accompanied by those similarly interested folks like yourself that you find along the way.

Be a Part of Something Greater

I am going to be a part of something far greater than that of a centric view. I will become whole because I am a part of All-That-Is.

Take the Initiative

I must take the initiative. The established elite will not. They think that they are born to privilege. In actuality, the masses support their exclusive access to privilege. I will help spread it around.

Imagine the World

Imagine the world the way you truly want it to be, and more! Do not be afraid to imagine. You must do this for the rest of us. Thank you.

The Word to Harmony

The word is to be heard. It promotes harmony the more that it is spoken.

Being Sentient

No tenet will exist that negates an entity for being sentient.

Received and Uttered

As we set into motion the word once received and uttered, increased clarity will follow.

Naturally Defined Justice

I am not concern that there is justice or not. There is always justice. However, justice is not according to what is artificially (man-made) defined, but according to what is naturally (ATI) defined.

Systems Not Considered

I am not interested in proving or disproving the system. I am interested in advancing my understanding and those who share my endeavors towards All-That-Is. Systems of beliefs that condemn will not be considered.

Violent Ways

I sense the executioner's violent tendencies. I will place myself in her path to stop her tendencies from going any further.

Observe

I will learn from a pentarchy prime constructionist what primes are all about. It requires that I observe her craft over a period of time. I will watch it take form and substance.

Sentient Treatments

I will stop terrorism here at home. I will treat all sentients with equal respect and dignity and the favorable pursuit of higher levels of awareness and truths.

A Chord Resonates

I will strike a chord that resonates for you.

Forward Movement

The message I am presenting is given to aid all for the coming events that are unfolding. The purpose is not to be overwhelmed. Rather, the purpose is to prepare and promote an effective movement forward. Your journey along the way will amaze you.

Promote the Spirit

Promote the (human) spirit. It is our path to ATI.

Escape Velocity

It is a thrill to reach escape velocity. I now understand.

Promote Sentient Environments

I will seek out umbrellas that no longer promote terrorism, but promote sentient environments.

One is Not the Only Occupant

One is not the only occupant on this planet. Join others for a more interesting experience.

Contents of a Time Capsule

I will not condemn you. Helping you is contingent on you not condemning anyone. Your other time capsule's contents of bad deeds can remain in it and be left behind. Do not release them in this time capsule if you wish to develop spiritually.

Start with the Foundation

I will start with the foundation (prime) and make it stable. That which is built on top of this foundation is just the way that I wanted it to be. It endures.

Following Your Lead

You will not be following me. I will be following your lead with your selection.

Sufficient Proofs

I do not need any further proof to know what is true. Some of you on the other hand are still seeking sufficient proofs to arrive at the same destination. I will go ahead and meet others who are not stuck in this abyss.

Prayer of Forgiveness

Forgive us for the diversion paths that we take in learning the word and the way back to whence we came. Allow us the chance to gain wisdom and knowledge of truths that existed for eons but have chosen not to remember or have forgotten. Help us to be in the word once more.

Prayer for Time

I pray that I may understand and live in your word in its entirety. Forgive me if I need time to learn its meaning.

In the Light of Your Word

I will learn to be in the light of your word. The word is for all those who wish to find it once again.

Worthy of Thy Word

It is with great joy that I have been given an opportunity to grow spiritually in a corporeal suit for a term of a lifetime. I know that advances to greater levels of awareness are possible. It is such a wondrous environment to develop in. I will take serious my stewardship in advancing a more wondrous environment with my thoughts, decisions, and actions. With these, I pray that I am worthy of thy Word and the spreading of the same. Amen.

Pass It On

> Pass on information.
> Pass on knowledge.
> Pass on awareness.

Love is Greatest

> Love is greater than hate.
> Love is greater than any mankind-made law.
> Love is the greatest element in understanding All-That-Is!

I will Listen for It

The word has always been with me. I will listen for it again and again. Each time that I listen to the word, I find myself understanding more of that from whence I came and beyond.

Prime Foundation and Beyond

Prime Foundation Specifications

This book provides general foundation specifications for duty caretakers of auspices prime libraries associated with any degree umbrella prime to operate as a starting point. The specifications can be extended to satisfy unique pentarchy prime challenges that arise in the intersecting paths of sentients.

Sentient Responsible Consortium

We are a sentient responsive consortium, not a political action one. This distinction will be readily refreshing in time.

Prime Construction

Do not be concern about convincing entities that are not interested in the framework of pentarchy primes. They will not be aware that a healing wave of prime construction is taking place in full view. The triumph is when prime directives will require them to comply or be removed from their positions and have their privileges withheld. Compliance will be swift at that time. By nourishing and promoting primes, we will have the most effective framework ever crafted for resolving issues arising from the intersections of members or groups of members with one another.

Nexus Prime at any Degree

Nexus prime can occur at any degree. With premiere founders, we will use the pent-degree pentarchy prime to be the Nexus Birth of Universal Directives. Each degree ascension prime thereafter will be to re-affirm or refine these directives. Failure by any member of society to comply will be noted and prime decisions recorded. It may appear that an entity is getting away with non-compliance. However in time, all debts will be cleared with compliance.

Nexus Fundamental Changes

Fundamental nexus tenets and principles can only be modified by the unanimous decision of the nexus prime leader caretakers and the plurality opinions of the degree minus-1 through minus-five of foundation primes within the nexus prime. With the event of having the unanimous opinion of the nexus prime leader caretakers, a significant tenet change request is made known to all. With the participation of the degree minus-1 through minus-five of foundation prime members within the nexus prime, the checks and balances are preserved.

Closing Remarks

Guidebook Ready!

This first book edition is written to be available when the time comes to evolve, as a society, to something greater. It may appear that much time has past and nothing is happening requiring this guidebook. However, the time will be ripe for the seeds described here to germinate. It will then catch on like wildfire.

It Starts With One

This book describes the establishment of an auspices prime library. This birth began with the sentient awareness of entities.

Living and Breathing Auspices Prime Libraries

Over time, this book will be a living and breathing one due to revisions that will be incorporated as a more complete set of nexus tenets and foundation principles is defined or established. These nexus tenets and foundation principles are ones that have been refined based on discovery and learning activities as we live and breath in attaining higher levels of sentient awareness.

Disclaimer

For those who need a disclaimer in order to continue to exist in their framework, any usage of pentarchy prime framework specified in manual scripts and books are based on the interpretation of the readers and users of them. This fact must be publicly stated. The author does not attest to any accurate interpretation made by any reader or user. Her actions are self-directing.

The Foresight Purview

This book is dedicated to all the founders who took actions to direct their own paths towards ensuring a most favorable environment for everyone to thrive and not the purview of only the few. We thank the founders for this foresight purview.

An Interesting Future

The books by this author are not about her. They are about the future. It is your future should you decide to make it a brighter and more interesting one.

Book Fund

A fund will be established to help pay for copies of this book in those cases when the interested person meets a hardship need level, which is defined as subsistence or below.

Primary Goal

The goal is for the Nexus Prime Instruments that are needed to be set up first prior to royalties from non-book purchases.

Towards Abolishment of

I will work towards the abolishment of terrorist laws and institutions.

A Hand in its Construction

This book, which is one of many guideposts, contains words that are set into motion with this publication. Some will view it with mockery. That is okay. These words will continue to be in motion and pass through time and space. One must understand that without the utterance of the words, then society's future cannot possibly get any brighter. Hence, the abyss or more of the same will continue when no utterances are forthcoming. Dare to hold onto the words. Your utterance of the words reinforces the framework they describe. You will then see the construction take form and substance. You will then gain the insight of having a hand in its construction all along. The words assist you to focus and see the future you are helping to create. It is a fine piece of work. Don't you think?

Directives of Prime Importance

Until the nexus prime at the pent-degree is established, this author will continue to write directives of prime importance in the absent of pentarchy prime directives. The objective is to reduce the transitional period towards a complete pentarchy prime framework.

Society of Self-determination

Pentarchy prime framework is not a political party. It is a vast societal pool of sentient entities resuming their right of self-determination.

If Allowed to Continued in Perpetuity

To continue the historical nation-state framework would have continued war, diseases, and famine in perpetuity by those elite feudal (war) lords that profit in material gains off the miseries of their feudal subjects in satisfying their needs.

The Benefits of Promoting Primes

By establishing and promoting primes, an entity will evolve towards a higher level of awareness, which eventually returns an entity to from whence she came.

To become a Monster

If one sustains a monster, one becomes that monster.

Changing Places

The events that are taking place today are ones whereby established entities are moving on so that more enlighten ones can move in to take their places. This is so that greater spiritual development activities can happen.

The View over Time

The questions will be asked why it took so long for the Word to be heard. Why delay evolution to a greater awareness? Those who vehemently block this greater awareness will not be viewed favorably in time. How do you want to be viewed over time?

Seeds that are Sown

For believers of historical systems, their destiny is not for me to choose. However, the seeds that are sown are of their own choosing. If we choose something else to be so, we can sow the seeds for more harmonious environments.

The Vision Solidified

Until the degree of separation from foundation prime is five or greater for the articulation of prime directives, many recommended directives conveyed by the author will be just that. Selection of leader caretakers is needed to codify prime directives. This is in regard to nexus principles and companion directives. The author asserts that her vision is in motion and will solidify.

Permanence

Some may say that I am promoting a pyramid scheme. How can you possibly say that? The model does not start from the top but from a solid foundation. The permanence is built on this foundation.

Afraid of What?

What are you who are non-pentarchy prime members afraid of? When you have decided for yourself, you will join a growth-promoting environment. When you continue to allow the elite to decide on your behalf, then you will continue to be a part of terror-promoting environments because the few who wish to retain their historical takeover-by-force asset holdings. What environment will you choose?

Individual Recognition

By promoting individualism by historical nation-states makes it possible to extinguish an entity. With pentarchy primes, a pool will have to be extinguished. This is a very great feat. Hence, there is safety in numbers.

The Outcome is Known

There may be efforts to silence me. However, the outcome is now known. Entities will stop terrorism by the entities who are pursuing developmental activities towards graduation. By their very nature, those who condemn do not have access to prime insights.

Self Holding Back

If you really want to follow primes, then you have to stop believing in terrorist states. If you cannot stop, then you are stuck in time. You are not even aware of your playback. You have free will to be stuck no longer. What is holding you back? Self!

Quantum Leap

Society will dramatically evolve by a quantum leap in the not too distant future. There will be no need or desire for feudal laws. After all, they are quite medieval to sentients.

Speak as One

I will be happy to be your spokesperson for our pentarchy prime directives. However, we must speak as one and take actions in unison. Anything less will prolong the implementation affect of our prime directives.

Exist No More

We must stop being terrorists and receive all sentients into our homes and hearts no matter where they are on this orbital planet and beyond. Terrorist states will exist no more.

Ending the Twenty-First Century

We start this Twenty-First century with feudal states promoting their terrorist agendas and will end the century with sentient centric pentarchy primes throughout.

Author's Birthright and Point of View

From this author's point of view, I am very uncomfortable being a member of a terrorist state. Some may say that it is my birthright. I choose to follow a different course. Care to join me?

The author's writings are to provide future sojourns the historical perspectives as to why it is not desirable to return to a framework of terrorist states. The future sojourns will hold on to sentient aspirations that promote the essences of being spiritually alive to ponder and to evolve even further.

A Sense of Awareness

Do not be surprise that others will keep their distances from you when they sense that you are at a higher level of awareness as you are now.

No One is a Property

No one is a property of any framework.

Do What is Best

Fellow sentients, you must do what you think is best. My hope is that you will also do what is wise.

Graduation

Your graduation is near!

Be a Founder

I am the scribe who is writing about the birth of primes. Development and awareness follows. Be a part of this spectacular birth and its unfolding. Be one of the founders.

Insight into ATI

By promoting primes, one will gain an insight into All-That-Is (ATI).

Belly of the Beast

In this case, the word must come from the belly of the beast.

Tear Down this Wall

To the Greatest Nation-State Triumvirate that has ever existed as viewed in historical reference, "Tear down this wall!"

Hear it Again

The word has been here since the beginning. We just need to hear it once again.

The Word to Pass On

It started with the Word. Now the Word is with you. Pass it on.

Bulletins

Revisions

Within a short period of time after the initial publishing of this book, the changes (refinements) will be found to be minimal. Over a longer period of time and after much discoveries and experiences, the refinements may be somewhat more significant. However, do not be surprised if the pentarchy prime framework and related tenets, principles, and instruments remain largely intact.

Living Foundation Guide

Minor revisions for this book are scheduled in five years of this book's published date. Input from prime members is welcomed and very much appreciated.

Comprehensive embellishments pertaining to this book is scheduled in twenty-five years of the original published date. I recommend that umbrella primes pend-degree and greater reach be the primary authors for the twenty-fifth year revision, which will most likely be expansions on the basic premise.

Your Feedback and Suggestions Welcomed Here

I welcome feedback and suggestions from any prime member. Your suggestions will be reviewed and may be incorporated in an updated version of this book five years from the original published date.

When feedback indicates certain passages of this book requires a greater degree of clarity, the addition of tenets, or the addition of prime guiding principles then a bulletin will be forthcoming so that there are no delays in disseminating this information. Should there be many bulletins, then an updated book will be published. It will be another twenty-five years whereby much will have been learned and articulated, at which time the author relinquishes authorship to the nexus prime umbrella.

Updated when Needed

This book will be updated when needed as retrieval and archival methods and procedures are expanded and refined. The aim of this book is to greatly reduce learning curves by auspice library duty caretakers and to share the best of efficiencies and the highest quality of preservation of prime directives for all that follow.

About The Author

Like other spiritual entities, the author has gone through life seeking a greater understanding regarding everything that surrounds her. Often times, much searching, studying, and thinking took place towards this greater understanding. It was not sufficient that she lead a comfortable life, but one that moves her closer to All-That-Is (ATI). Major life events tested her resolve in choosing not to be like sheep in going through the motions of a "normal" life. This notion was unacceptable. She chose instead to challenge the accepted dogma of the day and accept nothing less then a sentient awareness-promoting environment. With this understanding came responsibilities. Her calling became clear. It compelled her to pass on these insights to all that are receptive to this greater understanding. Her books are the culmination of decades of active pursuits in universal insights and how those wonderful insights can have practical application in promoting a sentient world.

www.ingramcontent.com/pod-product-compliance
Lightning Source LLC
Chambersburg PA
CBHW022249290526
45785CB00015B/475